The Spirit of Man
and
More Barnes' People

The Spirit of Man is a remarkable trilogy confronting the wayward power of religious faith. In three short plays, leaping from the Inquisition to seventeenth-century Ranters to nineteenth-century Polish Rabbis, the characters face a crisis of belief which calls for desperate strategies. With deep irony and ready humour, Barnes pursues his quest for scrupulous honesty in the face of the profoundly mysterious. **The Spirit of Man** was first shown on BBC Television in August 1989.

Also included are seven monologues, **More Barnes' People**, five of which were broadcast by BBC Radio 3 in December 1989 and January 1990. Nigel Andrew in *The Listener* said of **Billy and Me:** 'This was Barnes at full throttle, playing a dangerous game and getting away with it brilliantly, while also putting over some rich jokes.' And of **Slaughterman:** 'This bloodstreaked, freakishly comic sermon.' The seventh monologue, **A True-Born Englishman,** was banned for its references to the Royal Family.

Peter Barnes is a writer and director whose work includes **The Ruling Class,** Nottingham and Piccadilly Theatre, London (1969); **Leonardo's Last Supper** and **Noonday Demons,** Open Space Theatre (1969); **Lulu**, Nottingham Playhouse (1970); **The Bewitched,** Royal Shakespeare Company at the Aldwych Theatre, London (1974); **Laughter!**, Royal Court Theatre, London and **Red Noses**, Royal Shakespeare Company at the Barbican, London (1985). His television work includes **Revolutionary Witness**, BBC (1989). His play **Nobody Here But Us Chickens** was first broadcast on Channel 4 in 1989. He has also written numerous films and radio plays and has adapted and edited extensively for the theatre.

by the same author

THE RULING CLASS (Heinemann)
LEONARDO'S LAST SUPPER
NOONDAY DEMONS
THE BEWITCHED
LAUGHTER!
RED NOSES (Faber)
LULU
REVOLUTIONARY WITNESS and
NOBODY HERE BUT US CHICKENS

BARNES PLAYS: ONE
(The Ruling Class, Leonardo's Last Supper and Noonday Demons,
The Bewitched, Laughter! and Barnes' People: Eight Monologues)

Peter Barnes

The Spirit of Man
and
More Barnes' People:
Seven Monologues

METHUEN DRAMA

A METHUEN MODERN PLAY

First published in 1990 by Methuen Drama, Michelin House, 81 Fulham Road, London SW3 6RB and distributed in the United States of America by HEB Inc., 70 Court Street, Portsmouth, New Hampshire 03801.

A Hand Witch of the Second Stage copyright © 1990 by Peter Barnes
From Sleep and Shadow copyright © 1990 by Peter Barnes
The Night of the Sinhat Torah copyright © 1990 by Peter Barnes
Madame Zenobia copyright © 1990 by Peter Barnes
Slaughterman copyright © 1990 by Peter Barnes
The Road to Strome copyright © 1990 by Peter Barnes
Billy and Me copyright © 1990 by Peter Barnes
Losing Myself copyright © 1990 by Peter Barnes
Houdini's Heir copyright © 1990 by Peter Barnes
A True-Born Englishman copyright © 1990 by Peter Barnes
This collection copyright © 1990 Peter Barnes

A CIP catalogue record for this book may be obtained from the British Library.

ISBN 0 413 63130 3

The photograph on the front cover shows Nigel Hawthrone as the Reverend Jonathan Guerdon and Alan Rickman as Israel Yates in **From Sleep and Shadow**. © Chris Ridley, Radio Times.
The photograph of the author on the back cover is © Peter Bayliss.

Printed and bound in Great Britain by
Cox & Wyman Ltd, Cardiff Road, Reading

Caution

Contents

Introduction

I am, like all the others, trying to define the indefinable, fathom the unfathomable and screw the inscrutable.

I wanted **The Spirit of Man** to be about faith and language. Only language irrigates an event with a value that extends beyond the fact it merely exists; only language outlasts the dying it describes.

As for faith, **The Spirit of Man** is like the story of the rabidly anti-Christian Jew who asked for a Catholic Priest on his deathbed. The Priest received the old man into the Church and gave him the last rites. Afterwards, the old man's son asked him angrily, 'Why did you do it? You're a Jew who's always hated Christ. Now you're a Christian.' With his last breath the old man snarled, 'That's right, another one of the bastards less!'

Which reminds me of the story of Rabbi Zusia who, before he died said, 'When I face the celestial tribunal I shall not be asked why I was not Abraham, Jacob or Moses, but why I was not Rabbi Zusia.'

*   *   *

Why is real life always happening somewhere else, like the real music, jazz musicians are supposed to play after the customers have gone home?

I have had little experience dealing with the temptations of success. The BBC series **Barnes' People** finished in 1985 but the thought that they were more than eager to do another series had an effect. In the theatre no one is particularly eager, on principle, to do anything.

The knowledge of being wanted, produced **More Barnes' People**. It is not a return of Sherlock Holmes, however. I did not start out to do a second series. I wrote these monologues over a period of four years. Not for a particular series but because they forced themselves to be written.

However, would I have written them if there had been no one eager to produce them? I think I would but I am not certain.

One of the reasons I stopped the first series was that I was getting to know the medium too well. I was beginning to write pure radio. They fitted like a glove with no disturbing gaps between the work itself and the means of communication. It is usually more interesting to ignore the medium than to accommodate it, better if you make it conform to you, than you to it.

The cuckoo in the nest in this series is **A True-Born Englishman**. This monologue was submitted, bought, cast with the actor, Antony Sher, and scheduled. Then someone had the idea it should be first passed to higher authority for vetting. Naturally, once attention had been drawn to it, it was considered too dangerous to broadcast. If it had been produced, it is more than likely, it would have passed without comment. Instead it was banned, not because of politics, sex, or bad language, because neither politics, sex, bad or even good language are taken seriously enough in this country. No, the piece had references to royalty and that is something that *is* taken seriously in dreamland.

Mind you, the BBC do not see it quite like that. When I spoke to a producer about it he said, 'No, no, no, we're not banning **A True-Born Englishman**, we're just not doing it.'

I was perhaps too tolerant about the whole episode because I think I was secretly flattered. In England, art has no effect and very little meaning. So to create something, however small, that is disturbing enough to be banned, for whatever reason, is an achievement of a kind.

Peter Barnes, 1990

The Spirit of Man

I

A HAND WITCH OF THE SECOND STAGE

A Hand Witch of the Second Stage was first broadcast by BBC TV as the first part of the trio **The Spirit of Man** on 23 August 1989 with the following cast:

Father Nerval	Peter Bayliss
Marie Blin	Dilys Laye
Claude Delmas	Clive Merrison
Henri Mondor	John Turner

Produced by Richard Langridge
Directed by Peter Barnes

Darkness. A choir sings the majestic Dies Irae.

Quick fade up on a large prison, 1437 with a crucifix on one wall.
Marie Blin *is spreadeagled on a raised rack in the centre. The
Executioner,* **Henri Mondor,** *in a leather apron, stands to her right
with a brazier with hot irons in it and a large bucket beside him.* **Father
Nerval** *is seated on a podium to the left whilst the chief witness,*
Claude Delmas, *stands opposite, swaying backwards and forwards.*

Delmas Besom – besom – besom. Oh Yamma, Amma, Ahrsman,
she had a magical amulet marked with the seal of Solomon –
big – and the pentagram stamped on her forehead here, here,
here; hot needles riven up through brain parts, wrinkled warts
on the soul and all the time live toads lie hidden in the bread!
Raphael couldn't touch them, never, she was the Queen of
Egypt dancing backward to Jerusalem or wherever, the puki,
pooka and mashim, the seven signs of the Zodiac and men
cocking up their legs and women naked as the moon: bellies
floating off into the night, next week it'll be knees and elbows!
Oh, incubi and succubi, oh ki tu la puh SKILAR . . .

Mondor *throws water from the bucket over him.*

Nerval Master Delmas, this is a preliminary investigation into
the charge of witchcraft brought against Marie Blin and if it is
to end with the guilty verdict we all desire and passed on to
higher authority, you must deliver your testimony *soberly*. We
appreciate you've had a hard soul-jarring, seen down into the
Pit. But facts, give me facts, facts condemn the guilty. Give me
strict account and I'll give her strict justice. Where, when, how?
Dates, times, places.

Mondor Let me suck it out, rack, screws, hot irons.

Nerval Silence when you interrupt me, Master Mondor. Your
hour comes later. Dates, times, places, Master Delmas.

Delmas Date, October 31st, 1437. Time, midnight. Place, Lyon
Cemetery. I was on my way home from 'The Swan' tavern,
Father. I need that warm company of an evening since my wife
and children were pierced by plague worms, my crops blasted by
whirlwinds, my house consumed by Firebrands. God's Will be
done, though why He has to do it so completely to me is a
mystery. It's someone else, someone else, else, else is the cause!

They look at **Marie.**

Nerval It's my opinion that wherever evil is going on, women are at the bottom of it. Continue.

Delmas There was a mist that night, clouds across the moon but I saw what I saw – the accursed Marie Blin dancing over the graves. There were others but cloaked, masked, creeping round a cauldron, throwing in dead lizards, rat's tails and rock arsenic, besom – besom – besom. Oh Yamma, Amma, Ahrsman, puki pooka and mashim, SKILAR . . . (**Mondor** *throws more water over him.*) I was dragged over and saw Marie Blin anoint our hands and a pile of broomsticks with the cauldron's foul stuff. We put the broomsticks between our legs. Soul's doom, the brooms reared up, up and up, and we were night-flying across the face of the moon. She was leading. Down, down below was Lyon and the dark fields. Ahhh, I clung hard . . .

Mondor If God had wanted man to fly, he'd've given us wings.

Delmas An owl flew past me and perched on the end of Marie Blin's broom and they talked owl-talk. I heard them 'too-wit-too-wooing'. We circled Monterray Wood and started coming down . . . *eeee* . . . *eee* . . *ee* . . *ahh.*

Nerval What happened?

Delmas I hit a tree. When I picked myself up I saw we were in a clearing. There were some 30 men and women there, I couldn't see their faces but they were at a long table full of quarters of mutton, haunches of venison, sauce bowls of broth, plates of custard dainties and great bowls of wines. Some of the women were washing their feet in them.

Nerval In the wine? Horrible. Horrible. The Devil and Woman entered the world at the same time. Continue.

Delmas Yes, he was there. At the top of the table, between two naked girls was this huge black dog, baying at the moon.

Nerval What sort of dog?

Delmas Great Dane . . . or a German Shepherd . . . or it could've been a St Bernard.

Nerval No matter, it was *black*.

Delmas Black; absolutely black; blacker than black. Marie Blin rushed over to it and kissed its muzzle and the dog bit one of the girls on the right breast and left the mark of the pentagon on it and I saw it wasn't really a black dog baying at the moon but a green monkey.

Mondor A green monkey – that's a new one. But green's the Devil's colour.

Delmas It was preaching a Sabbat sermon. Nobody could hear what it said for it spoke a monkey growl but they all bowed to it and Marie Blin and the other Sorcerers rushed over and dragged me down to pay homage. And as they chanted the Liturgy of Hell, I saw a long crucifix on the ground which they made me walk on, whilst vice-haunted wantons cavorted and did spit on it – *spit – spit – spit*! I cried out for Christ's protection. Sweet Jesus, Sweet Jesus, save me in the name of the Father . . . As I was dragged nearer the green monkey, I saw it'd turned into a steaming goat with a devil's head. I was forced down, pressed down, 'gainst that hairy bottom *ugh – ugh – ugh*. My mouth burnt red-hot, my nostrils filled with sulphur-stench, *tu puzzi, tu puzzi* and Marie Blin spitting and the great goat King of Hell and Death, steaming and stinking. O Yamma, Amma, Ahrsman, puki pooka oh hi tu la puh SKILAR . . . (**Mondor** *throws more water over him.*) After that kiss, I swooned, cock-crowed and I was back in the empty graveyard, my throat aflame and in my head two hundred and thirty-four fire demons pounded iron anvils. I staggered up, glorying in God's infinite mercy and determined to expose this Archdeaconess of Hell, this leader of Sabbats, this witch, this Marie Blin.

Nerval Mother Church in her compassion grants the accuser and judge the right to the confiscated property of those condemned for sorcery. It will be but poor compensation for your night of tribulation, Master Delmas. However, you've done your duty and given us the hard facts we need to judge this woman guilty of witchcraft. Now, 'tis Master

Mondor's turn to do his duty, for she'll deny your facts and so must face immersion in water, boiling oil and purging fires.

Mondor Oh, the guilty deny their guilt always, Father. My instruments root out all such. Screws, saws, pincers, hot irons are tools of truth, God's tools for every turning rack-notch brings the sinner nearer to repentance, nearer to Paradise through pain. Pain, pain, there's only forgiveness on pain, blood and pain, pain and pain! SKILAR . . .

He empties the remains of the bucket of water over himself.

Nerval There's no escape for you, Marie Blin. No man or Devil can help you now. You hang alone against the power of the Church and State, which is set to crush you as a malignant growth. All that you say will be used against you. Marie Blin, you are accused of witchcraft, that you did worship the Devil. Do you deny the charge?

Marie No.

Nerval You were right, Master Mondor, the guilty always deny their guilt, 'tis what proves them guilty. Their Prince is the Prince of Liars, so they lie, lie and lie. Heat the irons, prepare the oil, I ask again, Marie Blin, in the Name of the Father, Son and Holy Ghost, do you practise the Black Arts? Are you a witch?

Marie Yes.

Nerval Mondor, the irons burn the truth out. (**Mondor** *selects an iron from the brazier.*) Marie Blin, you are to be delivered to the secular arm to be . . . What did you say?

Marie Yes.

Nerval Yes?

Marie Yes.

Nerval No, you didn't understand the question. I put it to you that you are an accursed witch.

Marie Yes.

Nerval You mean . . . yes . . . you are?

Marie Yes.

The men stare. **Mondor** *drops the sharp iron onto his foot in surprise, reacts and suppresses a great cry of pain.*

Mondor No . . . that answer comes later . . . (*He pulls the iron out of his foot and sways.*) After I've used the irons on you.

Marie I'll save you the trouble.

Mondor It's no trouble, I enjoy it.

Delmas (*gasping*) Then it was all real? . . . All true? . . .

Marie All real. All true.

He whips a bottle from his pocket and drinks furiously.

Nerval Ah, but as your Prince is still the Prince of Liars, how can I be sure you're telling the truth?

Marie You must take my word for it, there's no-one else who knows the truth.

Nerval No, there isn't.

Delmas What of me, Father? I know . . . time, dates, places. I was *there*.

Nerval You were also at 'The Swan' tavern, stone drunk . . . Marie Blin, are you confirming this man's midnight story?

Marie Yes.

Nerval Do you mean to hang there and tell me you flew on a broomstick . . . through the air . . . at night?

Delmas 'Too-wit-too-woo, too-wit-too-woo', don't forget the owl and the owl-talk.

Nerval So you talked to a passing owl, paid homage to a black St Bernard who turned into a green monkey and then a goat?

Marie Those are but commonplace at a Sabbat which we hold to exchange new curses, spells and incantations; they are ever changing. There's a fashion in evil as in all things and a sorcerer must be fashionable.

Delmas I flew . . . I flew . . .

Nerval If you were old and toothless, Mistress Blin, I'd say you were brain-blocked, moon-touched and babbling. However, you seem whole-brained and un-mooned.

Mondor This is no way to conduct a preliminary witch-trial, Father.

Nerval This is France, not Spain or Bohemia long gone in cruelty and witch-fever. We are here to seek the truth only.

Mondor To be the truth, it can only be hard earned, nicked from bone, torn from the mouth and metres of gut. Truth's never given free. 'Tis why Courts of Law are based on terror; truth is only heard when you hear the water on their knees splashing. 'Tis why my job is to rack and burn till the truth comes out from under. Let me do my job, break, rip, tear, gouge, brand and burn, burn, burn, *ahhhh*.

In his excitement he accidentally slaps a hot iron against his thigh.

Nerval You will please learn to bear your disappointment with Christian fortitude, Mondor.

Mondor Accomplices!

Nerval Cretinous oaf, shut and stump!

Mondor Father, she must have accomplices in evil. Names – we need their names. Pincers're best for name-getting.

Marie I'll give 'em to you without the need of pincers.

Mondor Have you no pride, woman? Put up some resistance. Where's your backbone? Show it to me and I'll break it.

Marie Cut me down and I'll tell you everything.

Nerval Master Mondor!

Mondor (*cutting her down*). It's a disgrace. Nobody's left this rack whole-bodied before – or at least ten centimetres taller. You're not even bleeding.

Marie *comes down from the rack.*

Delmas Now, she'll prove every word I said 'gainst her was true. I'm a poor man but honest, Father.

Nerval Marie Blin, you know the consequences of your confession of witchcraft? You'll be passed to Higher Authority, sentenced, staked, burnt, consigned to Hell.

Marie (*rubbing her wrists and hands*) It's where I've been all my life being a woman, it holds no terrors for me. Evil is eternal; a necessary evil. Without the Devil, there would be no God, without Judas what would've become of Jesus, who owes his crucifixion, resurrection and undying fame to that ginger-headed man. This is a darklin' world and the Prince of Darkness is its lawful Prince. Darkness is a force needed to make things grow. Plants would die exposed to perpetual sunlight. They need the darkness too. A woman, alone, twice widowed, I need protectors and the forces of the night are mine. Look around and see the power that rules men. I abandon myself to Lucifer. Damned, I felt the horned thing moving inside me, now violently, now silkily creeping. Oh, he glides a shiny serpent in my bosom, a toad dancing on my belly, a bat's pointed beak stealing kisses from my lips and in return by incantations, spells, conjurations, I slay infants yet in their mothers' wombs, blast the produce of the earth, grapevines and fruit trees, orchards and pastureland: men, women and beasts I deliver up to pain without pity. Sorceress of the Blackened Heath, Queen of the Dead, I have the key to Hell and I turn it. Oh, I turn it.

The three men make the sign of the cross.

Delmas 'Tis worse than I dreamed of.

Mondor Worse than I've taken out of tortured flesh.

Nerval Names. Give us the names of the others who followed you in foulness.

Delmas I was there but I couldn't see, a mist masked their faces, shadowed my opticals.

Marie We put the mist there for that very purpose.

Delmas Ah!

Marie But I know who was at the Sabbat. I sent out the invitations. Mark down their names.

Nerval No need. I can remember whole libraries. I was taught the Art of Memory by, er . . . Guiseppi Dun.

Marie Here follows the names of the witches and warlocks of the Lyon Sabbat in the Year of Our Lucifer 1437 . . . Jeanne d'Auvergne, Signoret Camnery, Edwige d'Bell, Françoise Amais . . .

Nerval But they are one and all high-born ladies, princesses of the blood, and Françoise Amais is even the mistress of the Prince of Lyon . . .

Marie Pierre Paternotre, Huguet Le Fevre, Georges Belotte, Leon Cahun and sons, Paul Daudet, Jules Breal.

Nerval But Maitre Breal is a magistrate and the others rich merchants, staunch pillars . . .

Marie Alfred Renard, Theophile Banville, Pierre Leautaud, Eugene Claudel.

Mondor But Eugene Claudel held the post of Chief Torturer and Executioner afore me. I was his apprentice eleven years. He taught me all I know today about the Art of Persuasion. Master of the hot and cold irons and what he could do with sharp pincers – pure magic! I rate him higher than Hammerhead Jacques, the Butcher of Arras. Claudel was solid rock all through. Never thought he'd turn to sin in darkness but then the best fall.

Marie They do . . . Bishops Chaville and Caynes, Abbi Verne, Father Arnaud, Archbishop Courteline of Nantes, Prince Ville of Tuscany, Duke Pascal of the Ardennes, the Duke of Burgundy and his Duchess, Blanche de Beaufort.

Nerval I'll hear no more!

Delmas I confirm it all! The mist clears and I see their long pale chinless faces, aristos down to their bejewelled boots, corrupt to their lace cuffs and spindles. You'll be coming into your own now, Master Mondor, spilling blue blood s'well as red.

Mondor And to think I'll have my old teacher in the tight clamps. He never truly appreciated just what I could do. Now he'll feel for himself. I'll map out a classic programme of torture to do him justice.

Nerval But the Duke of Burgundy . . . Bloody Burgundy himself.

Delmas Evil infects rich blood s'well as poor. Spill it, Mondor! Spill it!

Mondor I will. Till now I've only tackled the poor, sick and brain-gone. They were all broken before I broke 'em. Now I'll be breaking people worth breaking; the able-bodied, not scrawny wind-blown tassies. I'll cut masterpieces in their milk-pampered flesh, ripping silk, slashing furs, tearing delicate lace.

Delmas Rich pickings for us. The lands and possessions of those fine folk'll drop to us for denouncing. At best, I thought I'd grab half of Mistress Blin's holdings but now it's beyond the dreams of avarice.

Nerval No, this has dimensions. I cannot see Bloody Burgundy letting go or the Duke of Ardennes and certainly not the Archbishop. They won't let us pull 'em down, strip 'em bare.

Mondor They've been named, Father. Others being named are picked clean and thrown into the fire in the name of sweet Jesus.

Nerval They're above being named. They'll turn and name us for naming them. They have the power.

Delmas It's your duty to root out Lucifer, Father, wherever, whatever.

Nerval The price is too high. This confessed Mistress of Lies must be silenced. Rip out her tongue.

Marie Higher Authority will want to hear my confession, from my own lips. When I open 'em tongueless and I say 'uggh . . . ahhrrrr . . . ugghgghh . . .' they'll ask questions. 'Whose fault is it?' 'Did your knife slip, Master Mondor?' 'Is it a dark scheme to stop me talking?' You might silence me, Father Nerval, but what of Masters Delmas and Mondor? They know and though you force 'em to silence, what of that? Master Delmas in his cups, Mastor Mondor in the heat of his irons, may let slip the truth, that I named names and you suppressed 'em, perhaps because you, too, are a follower of Lucifer.

Nerval You devil!

Marie Thank you, professional compliments are always appreciated.

Nerval I'll confound your lies and prove no sane man would believe that list of names.

Delmas But I saw 'em. I believe,

Mondor And I! The top is touched with pitch and stinkin'. No one's innocent.

Nerval Who'll heed a tavern-drunk sonkie and muscled dolt whose brains melted in the fires long since?! I'll confound and confound your lies, Mistress Blin. Aside from their love of Christ, fear of damnation, why should the Dukes of Burgundy and the Ardennes and the Archbishop of Nantes and the rest crawl to foul Lucifer? Where's the gain? They have it all.

Marie All is not enough. How greedy men are. A thousand worlds are too few for them. They'd have them all at once and more too. Those proud princes wish to rule over the living and dead, the night and the stars, brute nature. Black magic gives it 'em, blacker than the black heart of Lucifer. So they gave their alliance to him in their blood, knowing Satan demands the bond be signed thus, for Christians are cunning cheats who make all sorts of promises, then leave him in the lurch.

Mondor They'd do that and more.

Delmas Nothing's too foul for the rich foul-smellers. They saddle the poor with Christ the Humble, whilst they stand fat and proud in jewels and furs, committing daily acts against God and man.

Marie When I saw the impotency of God, I, like them, renounced the Faith which was mine by the Sacrament of Baptism and now at the instigation of the Horned One, the Beloved of Mankind, Lucifer, we commit such deeds as he commands. In return he opens the secret gates to power that keeps the planets on their courses. Nothing is voiceless. The Devil hears his echo and his praise in all living and dead things. Unseen demons hurry up and down over the whole world when by the power of our art, we sorcerers command them, for they are our knotted and congealed vices which spring not from the stagnant air, but from our own enclosed flesh. Demons are our – your – weaknesses given Life, turned solid devil-flesh. The stronger our weaknesses, the more vital are our demons. We share the same demons, sorcerers and God-fearers alike. Father Nerval, you and I have a cluster of pride-demons named Sheytans; Master Delmas has his liquor-demons – little Mashims and Master Mondor, your demons are demons of cruelty and obedience called Devs and Tchorts. We of the Sabbat, Black Sorcerers all, control them and send them about to do our bidding. There are three classes of witches, three stages of progression in the Black Arts. The first and lowest stage is witch by incantation; those who invoke spells and incantations. Second stage witches are hand-witches, whose magic is performed by gestures of the hands, flexed fingers and subtle wrist. The third and highest stage, the supreme exponents of sorcery art, are the witches of pure thought, who need no words or gestures, but by their will alone move high mountains, pierce the heavens, turn the sky blood-red at noon. I myself am a hand witch of the second stage.

She makes a scooping gesture with her right hand and a large key appears in it. She holds it up. The **Others** *gasp.* **Mondor** *feels round his belt.*

Mondor It's the key to the cells!

Marie *throws it back to him.*

Marie I had my familiar, my pride-demon, Sheyton bring it to me when I beckoned. Lucifer's faithful have these other powers, outer and inner. They lift up their heads and waves of death come, towns lie ravaged, pestilence rages, Hell gapes. I'm but a witch of the second stage but I can still strip each of you bone-bare, see inside your fleshy worm-casing. My inner optic eye scans tripes, livers and beating hearts, burning like an arrow of pure light. It sees yours, Master Delmas.

Delmas You . . . see my . . . heart?

Marie 'Tisn't wax, but black and hard, bloody and cheating . . . I see it, and will hold it. I ask my Sheyton to bring your heart to me.

Delmas (*gasping*) No, it's mine . . . mine . . .

Marie Don't concern yourself, Master Delmas, your heart will be in good hands. Here he comes . . . watch . . . watch . . . careful, Sheyton . . . careful . . . don't let it slip. . . .

Delmas Nooooo . . .

Marie Ahh, I have it . . . hard . . . it's pin-size and hard but beating . . . See, I hold your beating heart . . . in the hollow of my hand . . .

Delmas (*gasping*) Father Nerval . . . Mondor . . . do something . . .

Mondor *and* **Nerval** *whip out their crucifixes and hold them up.*

Marie That will only help them a little, not you.

Delmas (*gasping*) Help me . . . me . . . me . . .

Marie I'll make you past helping . . . See the power of his name, L-u-c-i-f-e-r! I close my hand . . . slowly . . . round your beating heart . . .

Delmas (*gasping*) Feel . . . cold . . . fingers snatch at . . . my . . .

Marie I squeeze . . . squeeze . . . squeeze . . .

Gasping for breath, **Delmas** *clutches his chest and slides to the floor, whilst* **Nerval** *and* **Mondor** *frantically cross themselves.*

Nerval ⎫ In-the-name-of-the-Father-and-of-the-Son-and-of
Mondor ⎬ the-Holy . . .

As **Delmas** *gasps and croaks,* **Marie** *suddenly opens her right hand and makes a quick gesture as though throwing something at* **Delmas**.

Marie Here, take back your heart whilst it's still whole, uncracked. Breathe easy, Brother Delmas, it beats, it beats . . . (**Delmas** *stops gasping.*) 'Tis a bloody business squeezing hearts.

She holds up her right hand to show them the palm is covered with blood. **Nerval** *and* **Mondor** *shudder.* **Delmas** *staggers to his feet.*

Delmas Sonkers! . . . You gave me no protection!

Marie There is none 'gainst the fear inside. Lucifer Star-Maker, Star-Breaker, would break them.

Mindor Not me, not me, I have irons!

He rushes at **Marie** *waving an iron bar.* **Marie** *jerks up her hand and snaps her fingers.*

Marie Lucifer! . . . (**Mondor** *stops dead still.*) Your irons are feeble against the unseen irons wielded by my Lord Lucifer.

Nerval *holds his crucifix up higher.*

Nerval You've forgotten Christ, the power of Christ.

Marie A possible protection if you're strong enough and you remember him waking and sleeping. But time comes when you no longer stand guard, you sink into soul-dreams and sin. So weakness and wickedness come apace and I pounce when resistance is lowest, 2 a.m. death time. Then my little Sheyton slips inside and peels the skin back from your soul and lays it waste leaving you soulless at the throat of Hell, wandering across the marble deserts of Time, through Eternities without God. In Hell there's only everlasting Time and no cable of hope for Christ to draw you back up to him, no forgiveness, no redemption. I know, I've tasted it.

Delmas Ah-ah-ah what can we do?

Nerval Our duty.

Mondor The price is too high. You said so yourself, Father.

Nerval It's your damned cukish greed, Delmas, for this woman's goods!

Delmas It's not my fault I was right!

Mondor It's the cry I hear daily, 'It's not my fault.' It's always somebody's fault.

Nerval Condemn her and she'll blast our bodies, tear our living souls apart, God protect us. If He does and we survive, she'll name names and we'll face the wrath of Princes. The rich and powerful are less forgiving than Satan's Hell hordes.

Mondor Oh, calamity!

Delmas Oh ki – tu, SKILAR!

Marie Stop gibbering. It's 'gainst the articles of the Dark Sisterhood to show a trace of mercy – cover those traces, cover 'em, cover 'em! But just this once I'll unhook you from your doom, though the deed will weigh heavy 'gainst me should it be revealed. Lucifer would not be pleased. So swear by your pale God to stay silent.

Mondor
Nerval } We so swear!
Delmas

Marie You'll declare me innocent and I shall leave Lyon. Lyon is too petty for me.

Nerval Petty? It is petty . . . But how do I explain your innocence?

Marie Your sole witness was drunk. It was all the liquored dream of this walking sot-bucket.

Mondor That's true. Better than true, it's believable.

Marie In releasing me, you save yourself and gain the reputation of an impartial Judge. This will be seen as no blood-spattered Spanish witch-trial but a true French one, where reason prevailed and truth stood naked.

Delmas And me branded as a lying sot.

Mondor But you are.

Nerval Marie Blin, you are herewith declared innocent of witchcraft. The evidence brought by the witness, Claude Delmas, was but the swelling dreams of an ale-sodden brain. Thus truth prevails, Justice done, in the name of Jesus Christ, our Lord, amen. Go thy ways, Marie Blin.

He starts to make the sign of the cross over her but stops himself.

Marie Draw a moral from this, my masters – it's always safer to accuse innocent old crones, the poor, sick and defenceless, of Satanism and sorcery. Do not disturb true believers hidden like scorpions beneath the rocks. I am a backslider. Saving you shows I still have tatters of pity left but your true witches are truly vicious. Even death cannot stop their hate. They leave their teeth for pickaxes, their ribs for knives, their girdles for nooses and wholesale murder for a religion. Cross them and their hatred is everlasting to everlasting . . . Take this advice on pain of soul's doom, do not meddle with the Prince, the Demon of Death; do not hook Leviathan, the Beast, the Foul Dragon; run from the Angel of the Bottomless Pit; avoid, avoid the God of this World, the Tormentor, the Serpent, the Real Thing!

Marie *raises her fist but before she can bring it down,* **Mondor**, **Nerval** *and* **Delmas**, *rush out, knocking each other over in their terror.*

Marie *stares after them, then slowly opens her fist. She crosses herself and kneels.*

Marie In the Name of the Father, Son and Holy Ghost, I give thanks for this deliverance. You didn't help, Lord, but then you rarely do. But, at least, you gave me the wit to help myself. For that giving, I give thanks and these prayers. My only weapon 'gainst 'em was their belief in the Devil. I told them what they wanted to hear. If I'd denied being a witch, I'd've been sentenced and crisped in a day. The facts would've proved I was innocent but the facts are the least important part of a trial. So to survive I confirmed their prejudices, fear of the unknown, unseen; fear of the dark and the Satan in them. The fear that accused me, tried me, condemned me without hope of reprieve was the fear that freed me. So I say: to defeat Authority, use Authority's weapons.

> Do not deny their fear, increase it,
> Their fear, not your fear.
> Use it, it's there to be used.
> A cheap conjurer's trick with a stolen
>   key made them fearful.
> I cut my hand with it, showed them
>   my palm
> Covered with my blood, not heart's
>   blood, my blood.
> So they trembled at Satan's power.
> And when I squeezed my accuser's heart

I knew he already had trouble breathing
easy
Without my phantom squeezing.
Crude tricks, useless without words.
Words kill, create prisons
And the keys to unlock them.
Learn the use of words
And the abuse of words
And my hard words of advice
Dug out from a bone-hard life,
The only advice worth giving and getting.
For those about to be broken under
the wheel
Wit, cunning and endurance are more
important than heroism
Though heroism, in small doses, helps
too.

She laughs as we quickly fade out.

II

FROM SLEEP AND SHADOW

From Sleep and Shadow was first broadcast by BBC TV as the second part of the trio **The Spirit of Man** on 23 August 1989 with the following cast:

Abegail	Eleanor David
Reverend Jonathan Guerdon	Nigel Hawthorne
Israel Yates	Alan Rickman

Produced by Richard Langridge
Directed by Peter Barnes

Wedding bells ring out joyfully in the darkness.

Lights up on a bare room where the body of a young woman, **Abegail,**
*lies on a funeral bier in a wedding dress and veil. There is a wreath at
her feet and black candles on each corner of the bier.*

The **Reverend Jonathan Guerdon** *stands beside it, praying.*

Guerdon Soul-thorned, congealed with grief, a weed against
the wall, naught can reconcile me to her loss, not God, fate, the
interests of virtue or the hope of heaven, naught can ease my
heart-torn sorrows weeping forth this prayer on this my
wedding day, the Year of Our Lord 1656 . . . 'Rev Jonathan
Guerdon, doest thou take Abegail for thy wife? . . .' Eyes die
first seeing the foul deformity of death. I have lost my shield,
my health, saviour, pilot, bride. Why did He pluck thee from
me? Did I not keep your word, Lord, preach the Everlasting
Gospel? I fought on the side of right, brother against brother in
the Army of the Saints against the Royalist Anti-Christ, King
Charles and his pestilential minions, shouting the Lord's name
in the morning mists at Naseby, the place of dragons. Many
good men died there but we cleansed out the menstrual rags of
Rome with our blood and renewed England's Covenant with
God to bring order out of chaos. Yet I am punished for it:
Abegail is dead. And after the glorious victory, drum muted,
trumpet silent, the good Oliver, Lord Protector, plain Master
Cromwell to his friends, asked me to stay on his side for the
Commonwealth's sake. But the motion of the spirit made me
turn aside from this great honour. Men hanker after power but
I was not tempted by this world's baubles. I'd cast out pride
along with covetousness and the rest. Yet I am punished for it:
Abegail is dead. I became a simple pastor here in Southwark
who proclaimed the word truly, administered the Sacraments
nightly, maintained discipline strictly. Yet I am punished for it:
Abegail is dead. Lord, you struck your cold, pruning-knife into
that warm breast and her shining rays, so full of love, were
snuffed out. All else is base even the brightest love. She was so
fair, oh but, rotting black now, even as I weep. This is God's
revenge for some unknown sin. I ask forgiveness, Lord, and wait
and wait and wait again for the motion of the spirit. But
nothing moves in me.

The doors burst open and amid a blaze of piercing sunlight, **Israel Yates,** *with long hair and black coat, enters cracking nuts and throwing the shells on the floor.*

Yates You sent for me and I'm here! Israel-of-the-Ten-Tribes-No-Less-Yates . . . (*He bangs the door shut.*) Thy word called me away from preaching God's word, running up and down, staring at folk, gnashing my teeth and proclaiming the day of the Lord throughout London. Strange acts, friend Guerdon, confuting, plagueing, tormenting, skipping, leaping, dancing like a base fool, naked before women, *ah!* But God was in my mouth burning like an oven in me, setting my tongue aflame. God then fell into my pocket making me throw all my gold and silver onto the ground like these empty shells for love of Him.

Guerdon Brother Yates, I need thee. Abegail is dead.

Yates Now you are hot for me, before you were hot against me and other holy Ranters, simple men who only proclaim God's word, day and night as the spirit moves them, in the streets and market-places. Yet you persecute us up and down, up and down. You had me whipped out of Southwark, Brother Guerdon, called me a mad, bad blasphemer.

Guerdon And still do when you use profane language, are lax in conduct, enjoy bawdy, mixed dancing, singing extempore songs, wearing your hair shaggy, think Moses a mere conjuror and worse, say that God has told you that hats should be worn during prayers!

Yates They should! They should! If Christ would not take off his hat to his earthly father, Joseph, why should we to our Father in Heaven?

Guerdon Hats in prayer are blasphemy!

Yates But I'll wear 'em and still do all those things you speak of though less sprightly now as my bones winter. What day did I grow old, Brother Guerdon? No matter, I'm still able to rant with the best that God made all men from one mould, and this land, once lost to the rich and lordly, belongs to the poor and forgotten, forever and forever.

Guerdon We are of one mind there, Brother Yates. We fought side by side at Naseby against the King for that.

Yates And by that victory England is made a free Commonwealth.

Guerdon We swept away all vestige of kingly authority. And rightly. But you, Ranter, would sweep away all order, so things would fall into disorder like yourselves.

Yates Yes, everyone their own master, answering to no authority except the God in their hearts.

Guerdon Like the rest of your kind you are still a notorious ranting, Lord of Chaos, Israel Yates!

Yates Of-The-Ten-Tribes-No-Less-Yates. So why call on me, Brother Guerdon?

Guerdon It's a measure of my despair. In normal times I wouldn't have you in the house. But once we were comrades-in-arms in the glorious Army of the Saints.

Yates I've no time to talk of battles past when there are so many new ones to fight. We've seen Englishmen at last throw off the chains of slavish fear. But for how long? At heart they are a servile crew. They long to fawn and scrape and kiss the hands that keep 'em low. They fear freedom more than any chains and ache to bow down once more to lords and kings.

Guerdon Help me, Brother Yates! You are a sinner but you have the power to heal the sick.

Yates If I'm a sinner perhaps my power comes from the Devil?

Guerdon No matter God or Devil, heal my bride, Brother Yates. Heal her!

Yates Indeed there is no Heaven but women and no Hell but marriage.

Guerdon I am on the rack. Bring her back to me and you can have my soul!

Yates Keep it, it is too small.

Guerdon Bring her back to salavation, Israel.

Yates I've seen the bright lights in Buckinghamshire and Leicester but I've never seen a miracle.

Guerdon You've seen a King fall, a Commonwealth rise, and Englishmen standing upright and free.

Yates Yes, that is a miracle.

Guerdon Then heal my bride, Brother Yates. Israel-of-the-Ten-Tribes-No-Less.

Yates I cannot.

Guerdon I beg you.

Yates The dead are dead.

Guerdon *Aeeeeee.*

Yates Cry long, cry loud. Only Lazarus returned, the first and the last. And I don't believe he was truly dead. You need her, the Lord of Life claims her. She's Christ's bride now. No remission. Finis.

Guerdon *Aeeeeee.*

Yates You gather thorns not vines. Wide is the gate and broad the way that leadeth to destruction and the good always seem to go through it first. I've had five children – three boys, two girls and they died. Five pretty babes in a row . . . five . . . all five . . . five different mothers but it did not stop the Lord of Mercy taking them through destruction's gate!

Guerdon Did you cry?

Yates Whole seas. I told myself death is only a short-lived lie but it was no help. So I prayed. Have you prayed?

Guerdon Hard and long.

Yates Pray harder, longer. Do you believe that Christ lived and died and rose again?

Guerdon Yes.

Yates If you can believe that you can believe anything.

Guerdon Not this.

Yates Have the courage to pray again that she might live again!

They kneel.

Guerdon Lord God Almighty give us the word of life.

Yates In the name of Jesus who overthrew the grave, give us comfort. Let Abegail live.

Guerdon Let her live.

Yates Live!

Guerdon She does not move.

Yates You were right. All things are possible, but not this.

Guerdon *Aeeeeeee.*

Yates Not even the faith that feeds us can raise the dead, if they are truly dead.

He gets up, takes a handful of feathers from his pocket and drops them on **Abegail***'s face.*

Guerdon (*rising*) If they are truly dead? Is there hope in that 'if'?

Yates Perhaps she sleeps?

Guerdon You torment me with 'if' and 'perhaps'.

Yates In hard winters I've often encased myself in a sack of feathers to keep warm but they can be dangerous, they make you sneeze. How many larks and kingfishers have I missed because I sneezed?

Guerdon You lie, she lies still as death.

Yates Not her, the feathers, man. The feathers about her face. The rest are motionless, but those . . . See the faintest whisp of breath . . . one moves . . . there . . . there . . .

Guerdon A trick of the light . . . no . . . it rises . . . and falls . . . breath . . . it must be breath . . . her breath moves it. Lord of Life it is a miracle!

Yates Or bad eyesight.

Guerdon A single feather moves and I am knee deep in June. See, see, she lives and breathes!

Yates Breathes? – just. Lives? – that's a harder question . . . (*He removes the feathers from her face.*) Half-dead, in half-shadow. Catalepsy, Brother Guerdon. She's fallen into deep sleep.

Guerdon Sleep is a kind of death too. I've never trusted it. I say my goodbye to the sun nightly and tremble.

Yates I dreamed last night the prophet Elijah stopped me and claimed the world was coming to an end. When I objected he tried to sell me a box of figs. Of course we might have it all wrong. Perhaps we're truly asleep when we think we're awake, and those things that give us pleasure and pain are mere dreams?

Guerdon Can you wake her to dream?

Yates I must, else she'll sleep till Resurrection Day.

Guerdon Why you, not me? I love her and the power of love should bring her back to life and dreaming.

Yates As long as a man sees himself above other men he has limits and God cannot pour His holiness into him – for God is without limits. But I'm not proud, standing five foot ten in what's left of my stockings, curing carbuncles and hemorrhoids and capering up and down in the gutters of the world. And so God pours His glory into me.

Guerdon Wake her, and I'll caper in the gutters with you.

Yates *takes out a piece of quartz on a chain.*

Yates This quartz must pull her back. As the magnetised earth and all its bodies are attracted by lodestones in secret and invisible ways, so the polary power of this humble rock will attract the soul of Sister Abegail from shadow . . . (*He dangles the pendant over* **Abegail**'s *face.*) Fix your heart and mind on quartz, Brother Guerdon. Fix and move it. Together we will make it move . . . God's will through our wills . . . And so it begins . . . (*His hand remains still but the pendant trembles and starts to swing gently to and fro above her face.*) Now call her, Brother Guerdon . . . gently . . . gently . . . call her back . . .

Guerdon Abegail . . . Abegail . . . Abegail . . .

Yates Abegail, there's darkness above thee, below thee, darkness around thee . . . no world . . . no people . . . only empty corners . . . for the Lord hangeth this world on nothing and nothing is what and where you are . . . He sucks thee back, back, through endless night . . . Hear the sounds, Abegail? . . . A cock crows . . . a dog barks . . . Now see that single spark of light ahead . . . there, Abegail . . . there . . . It grows . . . Darkness lifts and the sun, the sun bursts through the last mists and see, oh see, the colours of our world . . . You are home!

Abegail *sits bolt upright.*

Guerdon Christ is merciful!

Yates His love shines like flowers on their stems.

Abegail *speaks in a strangely deep voice.*

Abegail Who raised me from the dead?

Yates Only Christ can raise the dead, so it follows you were but sleeping.

Abegail Died August 4th in the year of our Lord 1653. Noon, the sun shining through the bedroom window and the fields of wheat and the apples turning red.

Guerdon Sarah?

Abegail They gathered round my bed, watching my last breath, weeping, and my soul left me.

Guerdon Sarah! That's Sarah's voice.

Yates Sarah? Who's Sarah?

Guerdon My first wife.

Yates Your first wife?!

Guerdon She died August 4th, 1653. You've brought back the wrong one!

Yates Ah, yes . . . well, that can happen.

Abegail Who disturbs my rest?

Guerdon That's Sarah.

Yates She has possession then.

Guerdon Possession of who?

Yates Sister Abegail.

Guerdon Abegail is possessed by my first wife?

Yates Complete.

Guerdon Why didn't you tell me?

Yates How could I? I didn't know you had a first wife. I'm not privy to your domestic arrangements, Brother Guerdon.

Abegail Who disturbs my rest?

Guerdon No one, Sarah, it was Abegail we wished to disturb, not you.

Yates I see it plain now. It was Sarah who called Abegail to shadow on her wedding day; made her sleep and now takes her place here. We must discover why, else Abegail will be returned to sleep and sleep eternal.

Guerdon Sarah, 'twas God's will you died but Abegail cannot die on your will. She loved you as I loved you.

Yates *dangles the pendant in front of* **Abegail***'s face.*

Yates Please, Brother Guerdon, we have certain set ways of doing this. She'll only answer under the spell of quartz . . . Call to her, Brother Guerdon . . .

Guerdon Sarah . . . Sarah . . .

The pendant begins to swing gently to and fro.

Yates Sarah, answer your husband, Jonathan.

She answers in a deep voice.

Abegail Jonathan? . . . Jonathan? . . . Are you my husband Jonathan? Did you weep when I died? Yes, I saw thee weep and Abegail weep, holding my hand till it turned cold. How long did you weep, Jonathan? How long did the salt rivers run? How long, Abegail, till they froze? Was she still weeping, Jonathan, when you first kissed her?

Guerdon We wept as long as it was possible to weep, till the waters dried, and we could weep no more, Sarah.

Abegail I welcomed her into our home an orphan, raised her as our own daughter. You were away preaching and fighting to make a new land of this land for the Lord. Money scarce, prospects poor, as we suffered to endure. Then the pleasant beams of prosperity broke through the clouds between. Good years stretched ahead, years of ease. All lost, stolen from me. I had only the worst years, Jonathan.

Guerdon The best, Sarah. The years of struggle when we were up and doing, full of pith and purpose while the spirit shone in excellency around us. We were young! There's a word now – 'young'.

Abegail Young.

Yates Young . . . Lovely word, 'young'.

Guerdon Remember those years, Sarah, they were the good years. Years that can never be bettered, never come again.

Abegail I remember the April when God struck me down with the hot sweats. Abegail took on my duties as I lay stricken, gaining strength even as I was losing mine. She bloomed and I withered. I knew my death-day was near and my spirit grew heavy, husband, for we had so little time together . . .

Guerdon So little.

Abegail Yet you said love was a durable fire.

Guerdon Sarah.

Abegail Despite our love, I knew you would raise another in my place after my death. And it came to my heart that you would choose Abegail. She is so young, so fair . . .

Guerdon Sarah.

Abegail I grew envious as my last hour came and I called thee both to me and you saw me dying and your souls over-flowed with the sorrow of it. And I asked you to take an oath on the Holy Book would that thou would not marry Abegail. And you swore. And I died, my soul fled with rushing wings and my life-breath returned to the place from whence it came . . . But even before my shadow faded from the house you looked into her eyes as once you looked into mine, and you understood her as once you understood me and you could not let her go as once you could not let me go . . .

Guerdon Sarah.

Abegail And you pledged yourselves to each other, breaking your pledge to me, forgetting thy oath and my darkness. I could not lay quiet in my death. My strong will came to claim my rights and my spirit tore at Abegail's soul pulling her into sleep and shadow.

Guerdon Sarah, release her for our love's sake.

Abegail I keep her for our love's sake.

Yates So much cruelty and all for love's sake. Brother Guerdon, did you by word, act or thought, look on thy ward Abegail, profanely whilst Sarah lived?

Guerdon Never. I swear it. There is no deceit here to be brought to daylight. I feel no guilt because there is no guilt in me.

Yates *holds up the pendant in front of* **Abegail**'s *face. It swings.*

Yates Abegail! Look on this rock and come home. In the name of the god who dwells in you in darkness and in light, answer. Abegail! Did you look on Brother Guerdon whilst his wife, Sarah, lived?

Abegail (*lighter voice*) Never. I swear it.

Guerdon Abegail!

Yates Sarah, do thou know this to be true?

Abegail It's true. I know they did not look on each other whilst I was alive. But after I was gone, wishing to be together they broke their holy oath to me.

Guerdon Yes, we broke it.

Abegail (*lighter voice*) That is why I am guilty and so Satan drags me down. Sarah took me in as her child, gave me her home, made me her family. And I betrayed her love, broke my promise to her and God as Eve did in Eden. I am guilty.

Guerdon You are innocent.

Abegail Yet God punishes me.

Yates No, we do it to ourselves.

Guerdon You are not guilty, Abegail.

Abegail Yet there is no punishment harsh enough for me to suffer. Believe it.

Yates I never believe a mind in pain. Guilt and punishment, punishment and guilt. God is tired of guilt in every corner, punishment in every room. Why nurture tortures within thee? Sting 'em out! You have liberty to love and marry and nothing shall hinder you in this world or the next. Follow me! Follow me! Whoring is the essence of the joys this world affords and there is no human pleasure richer and truer so I've kissed and hugged the ladies and made the fiery chariot mount in me, without sin and guilt. Not a trace! Not a trace!

Abegail (*deeper voice*) You are ranting.

Yates And you are dead.

Sarah Justice. Give me justice. They betrayed my love.

Yates You are dead, Sarah. Justice is with the living. We owe no loyalty to the dead if it means betraying the living. For their sakes and your soul's sake, let Abegail go.

Sarah I suffer.

Yates It's natural.

Sarah I'm no longer loved.

Yates It's natural too. Time, not the heart puts an end to love. You are remembered with love. You cannot ask for more.

Sarah Oh it's hard, it's hard.

Yates It isn't easy . . . Light fights darkness, love – selfishness, life – death. So give liberty to the inward woman, Sarah. Let her go.

Sarah I can't. I want someone to blame!

Yates This is the hardest of all. There is no one to blame!

Sarah *Eeeeeeeeeee.*

Yates Let God speak and confirm it . . . (*He cups his hands round his mouth.*) Oh my children, my sweet Sister in Christ, I am God, the First Mover and am moved now to give my verdict . . . Abegail, you are not guilty. Sarah, let her go.

Sarah Why?

Yates Out of love, you poor fool.

He kisses her. She shudders convulsively.

Sarah Jon . . . a . . . th . . . an!

She slumps forward. **Guerdon** *catches her.*

Guerdon What have you done?

Yates Acted. It's by action whereby we shine in glory, Brother. So I acted.

Guerdon But does Abegail live or sleep forever?

Yates God knows.

Guerdon I know God knows but do you know?

Yates No.

Guerdon I know. Sarah's love was too strong. Abegail's gone back to dark and I am alone.

Abegail Jonathan . . .

Guerdon Abegail?

She gets up and speaks now in a lighter voice.

Abegail I was dressing before a mirror . . . thought of thee . . . and of Sarah . . . felt fingers round my heart . . . couldn't breathe . . . I was tired . . . Did I sleep, Jonathan?

Guerdon Deep but now you wake.

They embrace.

Yates When you slept, Sister Abegail, what did you see or hear?

Guerdon This is a friend, Master Israel-of-the-Ten-Tribes-No-Less-Yates, the Lord's true servant who wondrously guided thee back to life. You were sleeping near to death, Abegail, so we both ask did thou see or hear anything on the far side?

Yates Did God, the Master of Dreams and Death, transport you to far places? Did you travel through Egypt?

Guerdon Did you see Noah's Ark, Rachel's Tomb, and talk with the prophets?

Yates Did Moses stutter and Elijah come down on a rope or in his fiery chariot and show you all the heavens, worlds and spheres?

Guerdon Did you see Jerusalem?

Abegail No, only darkness . . . But now I come to think of it, I heard a voice. Such a voice. Oh my Brothers, a voice exultant, sweet and treasured, fine and true.

Guerdon }
Yates } God's voice?!

Abegail If the voice of Him who made the world has a voice, yes.

Guerdon What did He say?

Abegail 'Oh my child, my sweet Sister in Christ, I am God, the First Mover and am moved now to give my verdict. Abegail, you are not guilty. Sarah, let her go!'

Guerdon Oh, that was him.

Yates Yes, that was me.

Abegail That was you?

Yates You are disappointed?

Guerdon No, Abegail, it was still the voice of truth. You were judged innocent. There's no guilt in thee, Abegail.

Abegail No guilt in me?

Guerdon None.

Yates Whatever is done by you in light and love is light and lovely. No matter what the Scriptures, Saints or Churches say, if that within you does not condemn you, you shall not be condemned. So live and love and remember to praise the Lord with a full heart.

Guerdon Just as I'll remember to praise thee, Brother Yates. You have saved us both. If Abegail had stayed in that dark limbo, I too would have lost the light, despaired and died.

Abegail My love.

Guerdon So I'll proclaim thy worth through the streets of Southwark and the lanes of Middlesex.

Yates *stuffs the feathers back into his pocket.*

Yates Do not, Brother Guerdon. We've met in strange circumstances just as we live in strange times when people dreamed of infinite liberty.

Guerdon And building Heaven here on earth.

Yates Those coming after us will wonder if it happened, that Englishmen turned all things topsy-turvy seeing no reason why some should have so much and others so little.

Abegail And Mistress Joan Hoby of Colnbrooke could tell Archbishop Laud to his face, 'I do not care a pin or a fart for my Lord the Grace of Canterbury.'

Yates What days we have lived through, Brothers and Sisters. But they are already fading. And such ranting, holy imbeciles as Israel-of-the-Ten-Tribes-No-Less-Yates will soon be gone too. People's great desire now is to say nothing. They see their new won freedom taken from them one by one. But they do not care, Brother Guerdon, consumed by the greatest sin of all – indifference. They want to be left sitting in front of a warm fire, toasting their toes and purring. But my thorny conscience will never let me sit. The Commonwealth has no more use for my kind. We roused the people to throw off the old orders but new ones take their place. And we Ranters who cling to the bright light of liberty and love, are obsolete and worse dangerous, and must be pulled out by the roots. So stay clear of me, friends. I am of that company. Soon there is no safe place left for my kind.

Guerdon There will be one here.

Yates My thanks, Brother Jonathan, but offers of help wound the pride of those whose cause is lost.

Abegail What will you do?

Yates Continue to act. Without acting, no life, without life, no perfection.

Guerdon Call on us, Brother Israel-of-the-Ten-Tribes-No-Less and what you would have us do, we will do.

Abegail And gladly.

Yates 'Gladly'. That's a good word, Sister Abegail. To do things gladly lifts the heart. (*Singing.*) 'And there can be no happy glad-man, compared to a madman. For his mind is free of all care. His fits and fancies are above all mischances. And joy is his favourite fare. So be mad, mad, mad let's be. Nor shall the sad fiend be madder than me.'

Guerdon Brother Yates?

Abegail Are you well?

Yates I am shaking off melancholy soul-dust, Sister. Come join in. I would have you both sing-a-long with me.

Guerdon Sing-a-long?

Yates And caper too.

Guerdon Dance?!

Abegail But is it proper?

Guerdon I was rigid with righteousness but I've learned the only way to save your life is to sacrifice your reputation.

Yates All together now . . . (*Singing.*) 'We laugh at all wise men . . .

Slowly and awkwardly at first but with increasing confidence **Guerdon** *and* **Abegail** *join in singing and dancing.*

All (*singing*) 'We laugh at all wise men who really despise men. Their wisdom we always decline. Follow me and you'll see, what you say is frenzy. Is really but rapture divine. So be mad, mad, mad, let's be. Nor shall the sad fiend be madder than we . . .'

Quick fade out.

III

THE NIGHT OF THE SINHAT TORAH

The Night of the Sinhat Torah was first broadcast by BBC TV as the third part of the trio **The Spirit of Man** on 23 August 1989 with the following cast:

Seer of Lublin	Ian Cuthbertson
The Maggid of Kozhenitz	Harold Innocent
Rev Mendel of Riminov	Peter Jeffrey

Produced by Richard Langridge
Directed by Peter Barnes

A night sky.

1st Voice Let us worship fire.

2nd Voice No, better worship water, that puts out fire.

1st Voice Good, we'll worship water.

2nd Voice No, better worship clouds that carry water.

1st Voice We'll worship clouds.

2nd Voice No, better yet worship the wind that scatters clouds.

1st Voice We'll worship the wind.

2nd Voice No, better still worship man who withstands the wind.

1st Voice That's too much. I'll worship fire and throw you into it!

A Cantor chants Psalm XXII in Hebrew.

Lights up on a bare wooden House of Study with large darkened double windows and lit by big tallow candles in each corner.

The black-clad figures of the **Seer of Lublin** *and* **Rev Mendel of Riminov** *wait in the centre of the room. Behind them is a tall seven-branched candlestick with unlit black candles.*

The Maggid of Kozhenitz, *also in black, enters.*

Seer You are late.

Maggid They said I died last night but I don't believe it. I'm here as I promised I would be.

Seer Let us begin.

Each man steps forward and opens his mouth and shouts but there is no sound.

The unheard cry echoes in the far corners of the universe. This is the most important night in the history of the world, the Festival of the Sinhat Torah, Lublin 1812, when the laws of nature change, the axis of eternity shifts and mankind is finally redeemed. As the Seer of Lublin, descendant of Shelo, disciple of

Shelke, I lived seven years in silence, not wishing to abuse language; seven years with my eyes closed, not wishing to see what the world had to show me. Now they're open but I am still in darkness. So I've gathered my holy friends, Rev Mendel of Riminov and the Maggid of Kozhenitz here, to join me in this plot against You, the Lord God Almighty.

Mendel Locked in the habit of trusting in the triumph of right over wrong, living as if good will defeat evil when all things are against it and God hides His face from us, we find believing in you, Lord, is like climbing up a straight wall with nothing to hold on to.

Maggid Lord, Lord, how long have we known each other? So long it's been I don't like to count. Yet still the earth churns in blood and fury, cruelty and death. So let me ask You, is this the way You rule Your world? If it is, what am I still doing in it?

Mendel Lord, You looked at the world and found it good. I don't. I'm more demanding. I've no use for this world as it is except to wipe my tuchas on.

Maggid A fool looks at the lightning, the wise man on the landscape lit by it. We've prayed and waited but redemption hasn't come. Is it because we don't obey Your commandments? You knew we wouldn't when You gave them to us, but still You gave them. We can't bear the injustice of it in silence.

Seer We are going to make you speak to us and change it.

Maggid We know how. You've given us great powers, Lord. One day I was forced to inaugurate the Sabbath in an open field. A flock of sheep was in the pasture nearby. When I pronounced the hymn to greet the coming Sabbath the sheep rose on their hind legs to listen.

Mendel On a winter's day I went to the bath with a disciple. It was so cold icicles hung from the roof. But as soon as I stepped into the water it grew warm. We stood for a while until the candle began to splutter and go out. There were no others so I ordered my disciple to take an icicle from the roof, and light it. It burnt brightly.

Seer At noon one holy Sabbath I was sharing a meal with friends in Lizensk, eating soup from a communal bowl. On the eighth spoonful I suddenly tipped the bowl over shouting 'Trust the Almighty!' At that moment in Vienna the Emperor was about to sign a decree forcing young Jews into his army and at the same time I tipped over the soup the Emperor tipped over the ink-stand. The ink drowned his decree as the soup drowned my tablecloth. The Emperor said it was a bad omen and refused to sign the document. I upset the soup in Lizensk to upset the ink in Vienna.

Maggid See we've been given great powers, Lord, though they're weak compared to the Baal Shem Tov who could light the fire, say the prayer, know the place and so perform miracles. All we can do is say words, tell stories, sing and dance to gain the Lord's attention.

Mendel Before we can put our case, show Him the injustice of life, we must first gain God's attention. And we'll do it by singing, dancing, telling stories, saying words.

Seer Words were born from snow-white sheep. The frost wind is its own guardian and the hail wind is a messenger and the dwelling place of the dew-breeze is in the extreme ends of Heaven where Angels go down in the River of Fire to bathe forever and forever.

Maggid And the mountain shall dance and the face of the Angels glow with joy when He commanded there be lamps lit on the heavenly circles forever and forever.

Mendel For He has judged the secret things and by His oath the sea was created, likewise the winds, as the Sons of God chant His praises forever and forever.

Seer These are our words, Lord.

Silence.

Maggid God doesn't answer. Words do not attract his attention. And they were words of praise too, just as He likes them – thick and in buckets full. What does He want?

Mendel Stories. He wants stories. Here's one . . . Solomon once asked an old eagle what would happen to the world after they both died. 'One terrible winter,' replied the eagle, 'I was starving to death when I landed on a temple with a lead roof where a ceremony was in progress with men with long white beards. They saw me and someone shouted, "It's a hungry bird. Let's feed him." I was saved. Years later there was another terrible winter and I landed on a temple with a gold roof where a similar ceremony was being held. Only this time with men with long black beards. They saw me and someone shouted, "It's a hungry bird. He wants to share our food. Kill him!".' The world changes and usually for the worse . . . Come down, Lord, and change it for the better.

They look up.

Seer Mendel, Mendel, that story was too bitter.

Mendel Bitter? It was meant to be bitter.

Maggid Let me try. Wanting to punish his son, the king, his father, sent him into exile. The prince wandered for years suffering hunger and cold until the king finally relented and sent him a messenger who would grant him anything he wanted. 'What do you want?' the messenger asked. 'A piece of bread and a warm coat,' replied the prince. That's all he asked for. He'd forgotten he was a prince and could return to his father's palace . . . We all ask for too little from God and from life. We forget we are all princes in exile, Lord. Help us remember.

They look up.

Mendel No, no, that was too sad for the Lord.

Maggid Sad? I always thought it was beautiful.

Seer Let me tell Him my story. For months, the people of Chelm were driven mad by worry. They worried on getting up in the morning and going to bed at night and they worried about everything. So the Council held a meeting and a motion was passed to call in the local beggar Saul – the one who saw Baron Rothechild in a magnificent tomb in Frankfurt cemetery and said, 'Now that's what I call living.' Saul was to be employed at one rouble a week to do all the worrying for the whole of Chelm. Everyone was relieved until the Patriarch of Chelm asked a terrible question, 'Tell me please,' he said, 'if we gave Saul one rouble a week what the devil will he have to worry about? . . .' Come down, Lord, and wipe away our worry.

They look up.

Mendel God still doesn't answer. It was too funny, Jacob.

Maggid Our stories are either too bitter, too sad or too funny. He's very hard to please.

Seer That has always been the trouble.

Maggid We've failed with words and stories so we must try songs for one fragment of melody contains all the joy in the world and reverberates in the holy spheres.

Mendel I know very few songs. I could never hold a tune. When I tried some people called it singing, I called it neuralgia.

Seer In my youth I heard a sweet melody *The Beautiful Country Maid.*

Mendel I know that song. But it's hardly suitable.

Maggid We must sing *King of Kings*. In time, please.

He takes a tuning fork out of his pocket and hits it against his knuckles.

All (*singing*)

> 'King of Kings, God of Gods, wrap the
>   Heavens in His glory.
> See His beauty glow.
> All the trees rejoice, the grass exults.
> And when He speaks sweet perfumes flow.'

They look up.

Seer No answer. Perhaps we should have tried *The Beautiful Country Maid.*

Mendel Song does not stir him.

Maggid Yet the rock fish and the flounder sing, enjoying every kind of music except 'a catch'.

Seer We must try dancing. For the Universe is a dance and the rhythm of the dance determines the shape and pattern of Creation.

The three men softly chant the hymn Hitkabbezu mal akim zeh el zeh.

As they sing they produce Holy Scrolls from their coat pockets and dance with them. Jumping and whirling they hold the scrolls higher and higher and end with a great leap.

Panting hard, they look up.

Mendel Words, stories, songs and now dances are too weak to batter down the granite gates of His heart.

Seer We cannot even gain His attention.

Maggid Do not force us to use force, Lord.

Seer We swore we'd not shrink from it though it may snuff out our light and cast this world back into chaos.

Maggid Before we take that last step we must be certain the fault isn't within ourselves.

Mendel That's hard to know. Our God is a terrible God who seeks out our hairline faults and weaknesses.

Maggid Surely we three, above all others, have been tested and purged in the fires of faith.

Seer Yet one small part of our souls could still be stained by that last sin – pride.

Mendel No, I've singed and starved out pride.

Maggid And I have kept it from me.

Mendel If it lingers on in anyone, Jacob, it is in you.

Seer Me?!

Mendel You are the most famous of us, Jacob, therefore the most vulnerable to king-tyrant pride.

Maggid You've always been the most worldly of us, Jacob. And that's where pride has its home.

Seer No! When Rabbi Azriel Horowitz accused me of deluding the people with my holiness and told me I should declare I was not a saint, I agreed. Next day I proclaimed before the whole congregation I was indeed no saint, only a sinful man. The congregation chanted back, 'What humility!' 'What humbleness!' So is it my fault my fame increased? Then Horowitz said, 'You must show the people you aren't humble. Tell them you *are* a saint!' 'Never,' I replied. 'I refuse to lie.' Pride has left me, Mendel.

Mendel Nothing in nature is all of a piece and so pride prowls deep in humility. Jacob, perhaps God wanted you to proclaim yourself a saint knowing you weren't one. Yet you were too proud to lie for Him.

Seer That's very subtle . . . but true. Satan covets the humble, the conceited are already corrupt enough.

He falls on his knees.

Mendel You were tested as I was tested when my beloved son Nathan lay dying. The Lord wanted that sacrifice and I was wracked but ready, my tears washing out the gall in my heart. As I prayed the bedside candle finally guttered down to darkness. My Nathan lay still as death. But the flame suddenly flared up star-bright. Nathan stirred and called out my name. He had been saved and I rejoiced in the Lord.

Maggid But in the rejoicing you failed, showed weakness. God asked for the sacrifice of your son and then asked for a sacrifice even greater – to sacrifice your sacrifice. But you were too proud for that sacrifice.

Mendel That's even more subtle . . . but true. Instead of rejoicing at my sacrifice I rejoiced my son had been spared, I loved him so.

He falls on his knees.

Maggid I was tested young. I was fourteen when my father arranged a marriage for me with Sarah from Krasnograd. On the wedding eve I asked to see my bride. They were surprised but I quoted the Talmud and Sarah was brought, and lifted her veil and she was beautiful like a fawn. God spoke to me and I shivered. I couldn't marry her and I fled to another country weeping for the love I had lost for the love of God. I had been tested and was not found wanting. Later Sarah left her own people and married a Gentile. I had seen that betrayal in her sweet face and shivered.

Seer Perhaps you shivered at her beauty soon to be lost. You were too proud to see if you hadn't rejected her she wouldn't have married the Gentile and betrayed God.

Maggid That's subtle too . . . but also true.

He falls to his knees.

Mendel What are we but bundles of wet straw, three old fools, dreaming mad dreams in an obscure town in Eastern Europe, 1812.

Maggid We're flawed. We can't answer the simplest questions like when you knock a nail into the wall where does the mortar go or when you eat a bagel what happens to the hole?

Seer We are not the holiest of holy we thought we were . . . Yet we have the power to try to impose our will on all Creation.

They help each other up.

Mendel God doesn't compromise, neither should we. What is important is to accept the challenge.

Maggid Pharaoh too knew how to fight and when the blows fell he didn't give up. I'm less than dust but believe the Universe was created for me alone.

The three link hands and breathe deeply. Each in turn expels his breath loudly.

Mendel We now bring God Himself to Judgement.

A long note on a Zopha horn is heard.

Seer Let the palaces of Heaven quiver.

Maggid As we force open the gates.

Mendel And stand amid the cohorts of flame, girt with fire, crowned with light.

Suddenly the candles in the seven-branched candlestick all light spontaneously.

Maggid The Talmud speaks of 25 punishable offences. We charge You Almighty God with offence number 13: through Your acts You have caused men and women to curse God Almighty.

Mendel And they do it with reason for You have created a world where evil triumphs and goodness is crushed amid blood and cruelty and the closed heart never opens.

Maggid A world made in Your image where sickness, poverty, sorrow, mourning and trouble of all kinds are man's daily lot.

Seer So they curse You. The charge laid before Your representatives on earth is that You have caused men and women to curse thy name, Lord . . . What is your verdict?

Maggid Guilty.

Mendel Guilty.

Seer Guilty.

Maggid It's hard, Lord, but no harder than the verdict You have passed on all mankind.

Drumbeats.

Seer We three, the Seer of Lublin, the Rev Mendel, and the Maggid of Kozhenitz, now deliver our sentence – that You, Lord God Almighty, Creator of the Universe, be hereby excommunicated. You are excluded from the community of Thy children till the end of time.

Mendel
Maggid } That is the sentence of us all!
Seer

The drumbeats stop. The candles are suddenly snuffed out to a great sucking noise as a vast wind swirls through the room and bursts open the double windows and sweeps out into the dark.

Pitch blackness. No light. No sound. Then, as clouds drift slowly from the face of the moon, faint glimmers of light reveal the three men standing by the open window looking out at the night. Their hair has turned white.

They look up at the same night sky as the opening.

Maggid We've driven God away. We tried to imagine the world without God, now we know. And the horror is, it's just the same.

Mendel We've turned Him out but no one will notice the difference. For there is none. He never revealed Himself so who'll know He's no longer here? Only we know and no one will believe us.

Seer They did not believe us when we said He was here. So why should they believe us when we say He's gone? Nothing's changed.

Mendel It's the final end.

Maggid What do we do?

Seer Continue, of course.

A Cantor chants Psalm XXII in Hebrew as the lights slowly fade out.

More Barnes' People

Seven Monologues

The first six of the monologues, **More Barnes' People,** were presented by BBC Radio 3 in 1989 and 1990 with the following cast:

Madame Zenobia	Janet Suzman
Slaughterman	Ian Holm
The Road to Strome	Tom Conti
Billy and Me	Alan Rickman
Losing Myself	Jeremy Irons
Houdini's Heir	

Produced by Tracey Neale

The final monologue in this collection, **A True-Born Englishman**, was banned by the BBC.

MADAME ZENOBIA

Madame Zenobia See the Mount of Mercury, Bracelets of Life, Triangle of Mars, Girdle of Venus, lines of Heart and Head, the human hand is a map of life, a map yez'll never lose. Success, love, life, death, fulfilment 'tis all there, Dearie . . . (*The unseen* **Client** *grunts.*) Why be afraid of the future? If you know it yez can control it. Listen to me, I'm a Romany true, and used to be a Travelling Woman, County Wicklow, parts of Kildare, and me sister married a Travelling Fella, a dravvy shan down in Tipperary. When I was young we were out on the road with a caravan and a pony called Queenie that kicked the sun, moon, stars; she were as clever as meself. The roadside and hedgerows were our home, long roads and boreens all weather. Me father was a tinsmith wasn't he? We slept longer nor six, and even in hard times we always had a meal of an evening of cabbage and 'tatoes. There's where I learnt the Romany art of hand-reading. Some be born to see and more born not to see, there's inner and outer knowledge don't yez know; just as there are two ways to read hands, that's by the shape of the hands, or by the lines.

I learnt about the lines and cutting the cards from me mother, Lord have mercy on her. She knew everything but she didn't know I'd leave the road and stop. She'd smoke on her clay pipe and tell us things, threepence a pipe and an ounce of baccy, crying if she didn't get her smoke. One day she was in a Dublin tramcar and put the pipe in her mouth and the conductor says 'You can't smoke here.' 'I'm not smoking,' says me mother. 'But you've got your pipe in your mouth' says the conductor. 'Yes soor' replies me mother 'and I've got me feet in me boots but I'm not walking.' Full of back-cheek was me mother.

If her jaw was itchy she'd say one of the fellas is coming today, and if she saw a magpie in the morning she knew something was going to happen. She never let us have a day's illness begod. If yer was chesty she swore by brown paper and the wax of a blessed candle or a feather dipped in castor oil up the nose to pull out contagion.

Give me yez hands, Dearie. The left hand shows the character yers born with, the right hand shows the use yez'll make of it.

53

Yours is soft and well-kept. It's good to be so well-bred yer don't have to try. Indian fortune tellers read hands according to their softness. Yours haven't hardened yet. That happens when yez grow old. Ah begod, see yez index finger there, that's what we call the Jupiter finger. It's equal in length to yer third, yer Apollo finger there, which gives yez a balanced nature. Am I right . . . ? (*The* **Client** *is about to answer.*) No don't say anything, Dearie, let me do all the talking. That way yez can't accuse me of cheating, guessing all about you from yez answers. There was a time when I'd tell lies to the Pope to get money. Not now. There's no such tricks with Madame Zenobia, that's me professional name. Me given one is Bridget but you can call me Madame Z. Yez being a tourist and all you wouldn't have heard of me but I'm famous beyond Ballyknockin, Valleymount and Blessington. Sligo is the Devil's hole and Ballyknockin's worse but Tom would always say Blessington's one of the neatest towns in the ring of Ireland for if ye made a slip in the street of it, you was always sure to fall into a public house. A powerful drinker in his day, Tom. Me too, when the mood was on me. I've had a glass now, that's why I'm talking so, but rest easy it doesn't effect me powers to read the lines. No, I find it helps no end.

Let me look at yer Mount of Mars. There are two Mars Mounts, the active one, there, below the Mount of Jupiter, above the thumb, that one's well developed. It means yer courageous and yez got a bit of a temper when yer roused. Like me 'cause it's the devil of a red hair I had when I was a girl, shining like gold in a bog drain. Tom and me had tempers, and he'd tump me and I'd cut the daylight out of him: we put many a lump on each other. One time a judge says to me 'Can't you and your husband live together without fighting?' 'Not happily, sir,' I replies.

Yez broken Heart line shows a very demanding like nature, Dearie, and it's hard to please yer isn't that so? . . . (*A reluctant grunt of agreement from the* **Client**.) But yez well liked not only for yez appearance but for your honesty which is shown by yez good Mercury finger. When you show yer face anywhere you can always show it a second time, eh, Dearie? (*A quicker murmur of agreement from the* **Client**.) The Mount of the Sun is strong so

you have talent and beauty. Your home is a picture. Mine was
too. Women understand comfort better than men. I don't forget
to remember after years of travelling the road I wanted a room
of me own. There's nowhere private in a caravan, no place to
be alone, to cry. So I always had a craving in the back of me
mind to have a real home that didn't move on, even when I was
young and happy with Tom. He was never so drunk that he
didn't know what he was doing and never so sober that he did.
I didn't give a holla about anything but when I came into
somebody's house I'd say 'God, someday I'll be like this.' It's a
free life on the road travelling the land of green ginger, living
under the stars, but in the winter cold winds and rain bite bare
hands and arses, and in the summer heat yer firing away
vermin. We was married at sixteen in Dublin for sixpence by
Father Flynn. Me father made me silver wedding ring out of the
handle of a spoon. We didn't jump the hedge and run away and
not come back till morning like some travelling couples. Tom
asked me dad and he said 'If yez father's satisfied I'm satisfied
and Bridget is satisfied.' We did it all regular.

A dreadful hardship we had of it, people wouldn't give God
Almighty tuppence to take Him out of Hell. (*Singing.*) 'Life is
hard, Mother, Nights and days, Mother. Both hard things. Feel
life's stings, Mother. Life is hard, Mother. But there's no other.'
No cans for Tom to mend though he'd make 'em stauncher
than anyone. Bolts big enough to hold 'em so they'd never come
out. But what with the plastic they weren't needed ever again.
Once I looked out on the darklin' sky and said 'It's a night to
catch herrings, Tom. I wish we had a real home.' And Tom
said 'I wish for we had a half-a-million but what's the good of
dreaming when yer not asleep?'

But wishes are heard sometimes, aren't they, Dearie? Specially
if there's a star on the Mount of the Sun. We started trading
and dealing in horses and feathers. Some fellas'd give fifteen
pounds for feather ticks, same as a feather mattress now. Good
feathers was worth up to six pounds a stone then. We made
money on 'em, and there was this house in East Wicklow in a
bad state of repair, with the roof a-falling, and the wind
playing the harp through the rafters. We bought it for three
hundred pounds cash, and parked the caravan and Queenie

in the garden and I made it as warm as a rug, just like yours.

Let's look at yez Mount of Venus, there below the base of the thumb, there. Yez a great capacity for love and the dark stranger has come into your life already and yez mean everything to him . . . (*Surprised gasp from the* **Client**.) Yes it's love and why shouldn't he, yez a fine looking girleen, glowing like a greengage and there's great action in yer eyes. Yez has a strong Heart line not too long so what that means is yez not swept away . . . (*Amused grunt from the* **Client**.) Believe it. Look at my Heart line – see it's long and full of chains which means . . . Yer different. (*Satisfied grunt from the* **Client**.) All this is just a first general look see, yez understand, Dearie? I'll go into details later. Let's look at yez Fate line. Now when you make a wish, Christmas-time with a wish-bone, love, what do you wish for? . . . (*The* **Client** *is about to reply*.) . . . No, no, I'll tell you. Yez don't wish for 'things', cars, houses, jewellery or even money. Why should you, yez not poor. I can tell yez not poor without hands. The poor have an air. I know. I'm one who never watched her pocket 'cause there was never anything in it. No, yez wishes to be lucky didn't yez? . . . (*Exclamation of agreement*.) Well that wish is granted. There's a part of the hand called the Angle of Luck – there – the space between the end of the Heart line and the end of the Life line. The wider the space of the Angle, the luckier yez are. I've never seen one wider than yours, Dearie . . . (*Sceptical murmur from the* **Client**.) No, look, see how narrow mine is to yours. (*Grunt of appreciation from the* **Client**.) Luck gives you a sunlit future – like I had when we were living in the real house in East Wicklow. I got it cosy by degrees – furniture, paper and paint. We had luck with horse-trading, hawking, rabbit skinning, anything that turned money in. Some people get it too easy and spend it too soft but not us.

I think Tom was happy of it there. I never was as content as when I was staying in one place. I could've lived all my life there and lay me down there too. I knew where I was then. Now – níl a fhios agam cá bhfuilim – I don't know where I am. It was just Tom and me and me son Michael . . . Yez'll soon be rocking the cradle yeself in the space of three years . . .

(*Exclamation of surprise from the* **Client**.) Yes, you've got a high
firm Mount of Venus – that means love, marriage, home and
children. The Mount of Venus doesn't lie. And you've got
squares to protect you and triangles to make you lucky so you'll
be rocking the cradle. Like I did, though me lines were chained.
I loved Michael really and truly, I really did – a cush geal mo
chroí – bright pulse of me heart. I'd walk him to school of a
morning and then go to work like everybody else and collect
him again at three. I was afraid sometimes something might
happen and I'd no help for him.

There were clothes to wash and food to cook and stuff to clean
– homes aren't like caravans. I didn't have time to sit down.
Arrah they were good times, just like yez'll have, Dearie. Begod,
we're all on the razor-edge of luck. I thought I'd turned the
world around but you can't go against yez left hand. It's all in
the lines, chains, grilles, circles and crosses on the high Mount
of Saturn. Michael took sick one winter, double pneumonia, the
doctor said, but me mother was dead and her remedies not the
same without her healing hands. So my poor boy sank and the
doctor saying things to us and us not hearing nought but his
poor coughing day and night till I was left weeping over the
cold sod that covered him. (*Singing*.) 'Life is hard, Mother. But
there's no other.' Still go to Mass a Sunday but it knocked the
stuffing out of me. I was stone-made. He was where me life was
and now I'll go to me grave without a fight, say goodbye to the
whole world and let death cut through me bones . . . (*The*
Client *gives an embarrassed cough*.) Oh, no, no, whist, whist,
Dearie, nothing to worry on. It's only history. I was just telling
yez the story to show yez canna go against the left hand. It's all
set down here. If I'd kept on being a Travelling Woman,
followed the road and the hand lines my sweet gossoon might've
lived. For we never get pneumonia single or double, living under
the blue. Walls weaken us, Dearie. I should've known.

After the funeral we couldn't stay, the rooms moved in on us.
We closed the hall-door, hitched Queenie's daughter to the
roundy-top old caravan and took to the road again, travelling
the Emerald. Never went back to East Wicklow. The house is
bare bones now, the roof's fallen; all mildew and rubbish.
Ghosts walk there and I keep on moving and never the good of

a night since. People like me have to keep moving. Others with square hands stay rooted. Yez canna change it.

Yez won't want to, Dearie. Yez born Jupiter-fingered, that's joy-blessed. Yez know the good things and how to use 'em. I wish someone would put me a bird in the air but I've made me soul. Saturn was rising at my nativity but Jupiter's Mount rises higher with you. Yer's full of youth and confidence, everything'll turn out well. The squares protect yez goods, the triangles yez luck, the stars yez happiness. Yez'll never be in aloneness.

Now let me give yez real dates and details before yez cross me palm with silver. Everyone'll tell yez Madame Zenobia always likes to give value. I know I've been plattering on telling yez more about me and mine than yez and yours. But what do you expect, Dearie? I'm an Irish fortune-teller . . .

SLAUGHTERMAN

Ackerman After many years lecturing I've found students – I already know you too well to call you ladies and gentlemen – prefer the personal to the general, the concrete to the abstract. So in my opening lecture on belief and the function of reason, feeling and volition in producing faith, I propose to be nakedly autobiographical. This approach has always caused concern to certain members of the Faculty – but now I'm old and I've got veins between my fingers, and I walk around with my mouth and flies open, it's looked on as one more eccentricity. Absolute rubbish. I'm not eccentric and I'll kill anyone who says I am. I just believe you might begin to catch a glimpse of the bottomless paradoxes of faith if I first tell you about mine. Not how I acquired it, but how I lost it, which is equally instructive. I didn't have to acquire it because I was born with it, coming from a family of strict Orthodox Jews.

I had a holy calling even as a child and studied the Shulchan Aruch and the Commentaries under Rabbi Yakov Woolf with an unchildlike zeal. That's why I joyfully followed the tradition of my family and became a socket like my father and his father before him. It was my happy destiny to follow them and serve God all my days. A socket, by the way, is a master of the shechita; a slaughterer who kills according to the Law of Israel.

Most religions and sects have restrictions on their diet from the Pythagorans to the Hindus. Red mullet, now regarded as a delicacy, was proscribed by the Orphics because it was blood coloured and the Jews have an intricate web of prohibitions and taboos regarding the eating, butchering and slaughtering of meat. That's why they have slaughterers, trained in the shechita – in the religious way of death. They had to be men of true piety, who only killed with the light of Israel always in their eyes.

I can see a light in your eyes now: the light of disbelief. You don't believe me? Why? There's nothing intrinsically unbelievable in what I've told you. Stranger monsters than I roam the gentle groves of Academia – oh yes. The director of

Oriental Studies fought with Wingate and killed at least six
Japanese soldiers with his bare hands. Professor Hellor of the
Slavonic and East European Faculty is probably still in British
Intelligence – in more enlightened times he would be walled up
in the West Wing. Professor Saunders arm-wrestled the
Yorkshire Ripper and won and the Reverend Thomas J. Davies
is a close friend of the Sri Dera Ram Sukul and feels he has
touched the hemline of the unknown in his presence. There is
always a marked discrepancy between the milk in the coconut
and the hair on the shell.

Slaughterers, Jewish and Gentile, don't have to be big men, just
men with a sure hand and a quick eye. One blow cuts the
trachea, oesophagus, carolied arteries and jugular vein, *ahh*. The
knife's sharper than a surgeon's knife and flawless. I slaughtered
according to rules laid down by Moses, not by stunning or the
steel bolt through the skull, but the clean knife. One quick slash
across the trachea, oesophagus, carolied arteries and jugular,
ahh. According to custom, when I slaughtered a cow or bull
thus, I liberated its soul. I saw terror in the animal's eyes, the
blood rushing out like a sudden sea but I never once saw
soul-stuff leaving their bodies. Never once, but I still believed
my rabbinical teachers who said that Moses was instructed on
Sinai how to slaughter. I believed the Torah – 'Thou shalt kill
of thy herd and thy flock.' A religion has no claim to be called a
religion until it has killed something. Moses himself slaughtered
the Midianites under God's direct orders – animals it seems are
the least of it.

But Rabbi Woolf pointed out the sochet's knife is more than
just a killing blade. If someone is suddenly struck dumb, the
knife placed on their lips can make them speak again. That's
how holy the knife is. So when I went into my first
slaughterhouse it was like going into a temple; seeing the
stomachs, intestines, lungs and livers stacked in piles amid the
steam of the great carcasses being axed in two, didn't change it.
The animals bellowed and struggled and revealed the teachings
of the Torah, as we turned livestock into dead-stock. Still they
expired in blood and excrement. There's nothing particularly
bestial about dying like that. The Emperor Claudius's last
words as he died after he'd broken wind, watching a troupe

of comics, was, 'Oh dear, oh dear, I think I've done a
mess.'

I slaughtered by day and studied the Torah by night. The
Torah which created angels and worlds and is the root principal
of all. Like the Koran it is a sacred book. The Supreme Being
condescended to producing a book which is rather more
incredible than Him condescending to become a man. In the
Torah nothing is accidental. God, whose words are the
instrument of His work, created the world through words. God
said 'Let there be light,' and there was light. If He had said
another word then the result would've been different. He
could've said 'Let there be soap,' or 'Let there be kraplash'.
Then where would we've been?

In my night studies I learned the mysteries of the Consuming
Fire and the six hundred and thirteen limbs of man's spiritual
body. There was no darkness in my nights, no slaughtering, no
blood, spleen, liver or lights – only the light from the Throne of
Light. I lived in the higher world by night and the world of
deeds by day. But I saw no separation between day and night,
pure spirit, dead flesh: all was one. By seeing God in all things,
even in the killing yards, I saw through the veil of separation
that keeps Him from us.

That's what is called faith. It should've weakened in the
slaughterhouse for no one else saw the divine sparks I saw
there. All was cheating, stealing, petty meanness. The butchers
talked of money and women as they chopped heads in two and
skinned 'em even before the carcasses breathed their last
breath. They never looked up. When one of them was told his
wife had just given birth to a ten pound boy he said absently,
'With or without bones?'. But sinking into that lower world
only strengthened my faith in the higher. Faith thrives on
adversity.

My father, however, was affected in the end. All necks began to
remind him of the knife. Men and women, like birds and beasts,
had guts and giblets too, and one slash made them all dead
meat. He drank heavily to cheer himself up. In his dreams all
kinds of animals with slit throats and flayed hides cursed him in
Hebrew and shouted, 'We're not Jewish.'

One day before he died I found him reading the Kabbalah. He was much taken with the idea of the Eternal Being and His emanations. In the beginning there was a Supreme Being and from Him emanated another god and from that emanation another and from that another. There were three hundred and sixty-five gods in all. When we reach the final three hundred and sixty-fifth god the divine part had been reduced to almost zero – this god was called Jehovah who created the world. That's why it's so full of guilt and blood, because Jehovah had so little of the divine left in Him. This explanation seemed to calm my father a little. But not enough. To die of drunkenness after spending a carefree life, though deplored by the world, need not be an unhappy close but to die drunk and in despair is a bad end. Yet it didn't cause me to question my belief or my calling. For man cannot allow himself to be more compassionate than God who says 'Kill my creatures and eat.'

If the Baal Shem could have met Rabbi Haim Ben Atar in the Holy Land where he was waiting for him, they could've hastened the coming of the Messiah. Hassidic tradition says every encounter quickens the steps of the Redeemer; let two beings meet and accept one another and the world is no longer the same. My encounter happened in Elul, the Jewish New Year. It's a busy time for any sochet. So much meat is needed, the killing yards are crammed with food on the hoof. There was nothing to say that cow was going to be different from any of the others I'd killed that morning. She waited behind the gate, her hind leg attached to a chain. When it was her turn, her hind leg was pulled rigid by her own weight as she was hoisted up above the gate, first the legs, then the torso, then the head. As she started mooing in terror I slashed her across the neck beneath the mandible. Her blood gushed out making her body twist on the end of the chain and the torrent soon became a trickle.

It was a perfect execution. As I put my hand up to stop her final twitching, I touched the belly and felt something. I pressed my ear against her stomach. There was something moving in her. I was as surprised as Pope Pius XII must have been when he had the catacombs of St Peter's opened hoping to find the remains of the Prince of Apostles and came up with the face of Dionysus instead.

Without thinking I took my knife and slit open the cow's stomach, plunged my hands inside the womb and helped out a new-born calf. It stood there wet on wobbly legs, looking round wide-eyed at the scene of carnage it had been born into.

How a pregnant cow passed inspection was a mystery and how I came to pluck out the calf is an even bigger one. A stupid thing to do. I had no business behaving like that. But it was at that moment my heart saw what my hand had been made to do. Mankind's true moral test consists of its attitude towards those who are at its mercy – animals. And in this respect mankind has suffered a fundamental disaster, so fundamental that all other disasters spring from it. I didn't think that then, as the new-born calf and I stared at each other in the steam and the butchers stared at both of us. But I do remember thinking that the cover of the holy Torah was covered with dead meat, calves' skin. God was a butcher too but I didn't want to do His dirty work for Him any more: surely life was better than death? So I took off my skull-cap and apron and dropped my knife and left with the calf.

I never went back to that place or the beliefs that had led me to work there. I'd climbed to the top of the mast and when I came down the ship had gone. It's as easy to lose your faith as gain it and it can happen in an instant, in a cloud of unknowing.

According to the Master of Zen, finding the truth through sudden intuition requires a sudden shock, something beyond logic. You ask a question and the Master gives you an illogical answer. 'What is the Buddha?' 'Three pounds of stoneless cherries.' These words contain no allegorical meaning. Their meaning is in their meaninglessness. Sometimes the answer may be a blow, mine was the appearance of a live calf from a dead cow.

I'm not an atheist, atheists get no holidays, but if I could I'd write in every synagogue, church, mosque, or temple the line 'Important if true.' Does that mean I'm an agnostic? I don't know. I do know the slaughterhouse calf changed me completely. I didn't behave like Nimrod who challenged the

Almighty and fired an arrow at the sky and it came back covered with blood, but now I prefer the antics of a duck trying to scratch its neck with its foot than anything Elijah could show me in Heaven.

I came to the conclusion that all the big ideas about God, faith and grace were for playing with and not for committing myself to. I felt there was every chance they answered nothing in this soulless universe. And so I became an academic and retired from this accursed world.

Of course we all believe in something. My Janitor, who I respect, above many of my colleagues, believes he had a better theory of evolution than the Big Bang. 'There's a huge tortoise, with a thin covering of earth on its back and that's the universe.' 'But what is the tortoise standing on, John?' 'On a bigger tortoise, of course. It's no use arguing, Mr Ackerman, it's tortoises all the way down.' On the other hand, Cardinal Richelieu's sister didn't dare sit because she believed she was made of glass. Then again the Macedonian armies of the fourth century believed they were purified by marching between the two halves of a severed dog and many Christians believed Christ was born out of his mother's left ear.

If you don't believe this story of mine it's no great matter, at least it held your attention. But why shouldn't you believe it? Why shouldn't you? If Hindus believe the Himalayas are Shiva's mule, why shouldn't you believe, at one time, I was a full-time slaughterman? Just have a little faith. No questions, please.

THE ROAD TO STROME

James Drummond *falls, gasping loudly.*

Drummond Swirlishoo . . . swirlishoo . . . the sea . . . the sea
. . . pu doon herrin? . . . dark hood owre mae eens . . . tysties in
the sky . . . mountains on mae chest, Aonach Mor and Stob
Dearg . . . I'm on the edge of the Main Deep, Mary . . . there's
a braw wind blowing . . . but it's all blethers, blathers and
clytach . . . (*Chuckling painfully.*) A parachutist jumps, pulls the
cord and nocht happens. As he falls he gleans another man
shooting oop alow him. As they pass the wee parachutist yowls:
'Do yer ken anything about parachutes?' The other man yowls
back: 'No! Do yer ken anything aboot gas-cookers?' . . .
(*Chuckles painfully.*) Keep smiling Jamie laddie, keep smiling . . .
All pleasure comes from Paradise e'en jokes but windows are a
mystery . . . time tae burn the witch with the crew on the
fishing grounds going aboot the deck burning pieces o' paper
tae bring us luck . . . I'm no afeered of dying, gowpin' up mae
hert here on the road tae Strome, by a hawthorn bush and nae
a soul in sight . . . I cannae send fer a doctor so I'll dei a
natural death . . . Heart attacks are very natural not like poor
Robbie McKyle, hit by a jib and over the side . . . we laid
evens he'd be dead within the hour and he was. 'And if ye get
that skrimshanker Willie Patterson tae make mae coffin I'll no
put a foot in it,' he said when we fished him out the sea . . . I'd
like tae get home afore I dei . . . Keep blathering, Jamie. If yer
can still hear the sound of yer ain voice then yir still alive, man
. . . sae make murgeons wi' yer mooth . . . keep blathering and
blethering, yabbin' and yammerin' . . . Snailie, snailie, shoot oot
yer horn. An' tell me if it will be a bonny day the morn.
(*Singing.*) 'The moudiewort, the moudiewort, The mumpin beast
the moudiewort, The crows thae pykit the moudiewort, The
puir wee beast the moudiewort.'

On the day of creation when the Lord was shooting His nets,
making this warl', one of the Angels looked doon at it and quo'
'All the people are weeping.' The Lord replied, 'Then it's no the
warl' yet.' . . . Next day the Angel looked down again, 'Now all
the people are laughing.' 'Then it's no the warl' yet,' replied the

Lord. The Angel looked doon on the third day. 'Now some people are weeping, some laughing.' 'Now it's the warl'!' replied the Lord. For in the warl' one weeps, another laughs. I'm singing tae the herrin's, Mary . . . You've luck, Jamie, sure death'd catch you cold at sea drowning five fathoms deep or worse in 'jamas and an ear-trumpet . . . Mae Mary should've deid like this, said goodbye tae the white warl', larks crying 'Guid morning, Mary. Guid morning.' Now I sigh and say ye are nae longer mae Mary Morrison . . . Oh a luvin' wumman's like a licht, come awa mae lass, mae lassie, come awa, come awa . . . Keep yammerin', Jamie. 'The horny-goloch is an awesome beast. Soople an scaly. It has twa horns, an' a hantle o' feet. An' a forkie tailie' . . .

Feel the wind in mae face, Mary . . . and we're sailing due West . . . Look at those ravens owre there – birds o' ill omen. They're no' ravens, they're pigeons. Well mebbe they're omen-pigeons . . . (*He chuckles.*) Why should I be afeered o' dying? Minister Kilbride said ''Tis impossible for a rich man tae enter the Kingdom of Heaven as fer a coo tae climb a tree wi' her tail forward or a sow tae sit on a thistle and whistle like a mavis.' That lets me in. I've been poor all mae days, never seen rich.

Being puir wasnae enough fer Minister Kilbride wi' a face like the Day o' Judgement. Delivering the Word amongst us he knocked three pulpits all tae shivers and dung the guts out o' five bibles. 'Lord dibble the kail seed o' Thy Grace into our herts and if we cannae grow oop good kail make us, at least, good sprouts. And ha' mercy on yon wee sinner Jamie Drummond afore he causes us all a further load o' stramash.'

I had a taste fer the barley bree with a text hanging on mae bedroom wall saying 'Help all ye that thirsteth'. But I never took mae whisky neat, always diluted it wi' vodka, dinnae I, Mary? Recall coming home drunk, full tae the gills one moonlight nicht and falling into a stream ootside our house – how can the moon move the waves, Mary, but stones cannae be turned an inch either way? Anyway I looks doon and saw the moon skimmerin' there in the water. I yowled 'Mary, Mary!' She yowled back 'Where are yer, Jamie?' 'Guidness knows where I am, but I ken I'm somewhere faur above the moon,' I says and she comes oot laughing like a loon.

The wummen . . . the wummen . . . all the bonnie wummen in their bright green gowns, breasts like starnies, arms like young willows. Poverty makes beautiful wummen ugly but not mae Mary. Wi' the devil aways in mae brecks I had the devil o' a reputation when I was young . . . a braw fisherman o' herrin's and wummen. I thought nae more o' committing sin than a dog does o' lickin' a dish. Och but it was all a penny whistle . . . small stuff . . . small stuff. Och how I'd sing tae the wummen and the herrin' wi' a kind o' lilt wi' nae tune tae it but it'd charm the fish and the wummen into mae net. (*Singing*.) 'Dance tae yer daddy Ma bonnie wee lassie Dance tae yer daddy Mae bonnie wee lamb.'

Once Strome was full o' people; Bruce Mackie the virtuoso o' the tin whistle . . . Bobby Tutt, champion whisky drinker o' all Scotland . . . Alex Twine, the eighty-year-old muscle man from Caithness. He never went any place he couldnae take his wife. Puir man, there's little chance of him going tae Heaven. The herrin' fleets have gone tae. The auld brown-sailed drifters driven out by the steamers shooting their nets and getting the catch home first. I've sailed the length o' Britain wi' the Strome fleet . . . far as Comul waters . . . and tae the gutting stations at Collaforth. Mary was one o' the bricht lassies there . . . cut and gut bonnie lassies, bonnie lassies . . . 'I wish I were where Mary lies. Night and day on me she cries. O that I were where Mary lies. On fair Kirkconnel lea.' All gone. Young Jimmy Hendry the boy who cooked fer the crew and Robbie who went over the side and his brother Laurie who was lost tae . . . all the men lost and the boats broken . . . sands filled wi' the skulls and bones o' drowned fishermen moaning tae God. 'Lord, Lord, we dunnae nag at ye like Methodists. We're quiet, hard workin' fishermen and if you'll only keep us from drownin' this time we'll no' bother you again fer a guid long while.'

With the fleet gone Mary and me went tae. The sea could no longer provide us wi' a living so we concerned ourself with dryland things, Glasgow and the warl' o' stones . . . helping build ships I'd never sail, iron gates shut behind mae back, a drudge o' steel and daylong murk . . . Coming home years later,

Strome was full o' ghosts. Little Maggie Ross fell out o' bed
and deid in April aged ten dinnae she? A week later Fergus the
milkman saw her standing in front o' the Kirk. 'What're yer
doing here, lassie? Yer deid,' says Fergus. Fergus was a
Scotsman straight off the oatmeal pack, skirl-in-the-pan,
skirl-in-the-pan! 'Deid? What's deid?' asked the deid girl. 'Weel
deid's deid,' replies Fergus. 'Who says?' says the girl. 'Doctors!'
came the reply. 'Och what dae doctors ken?' says the wee lassie
and vanishes.

Try tae sit oop, Jamie . . . pull yerself oop . . . I ken it all. I've
had a heart-attack afore haven't I? Falling in the parlour
suffocating in a snowstorm yowlin' 'Put the floor back under the
carpet, Mary!' Now it's death on this deasie road wi' no Mary
tae see me through . . . when I loved her I walked so light ma
feet barely touched the ground . . . Tae little and tae late . . .

They thought I was deid. Stuck a goose-feather oop mae snout
and it dinnae stir. At the hospital it was 'Deid on arrival' wi'
Mary weeping, eens red wi' weeping. There's a tombstone in
Strome cemetery wi' the words: 'They wouldnae believe me
when I said mae feet were killing me.'

I'd heard the lone piper play so they layed me doon tae be
wrapped and slid awa' oot the back. There I was, stiff and
gorded, deid and deasie. Then suddenly I sneezed and sat up.
Och what dae doctors ken?

Ease yerself oop, Jamie . . . off the road . . . else yer'll be
knocked doon by a passing yak. Hard country, sandstone and
quartzite, empty 'cept for Scots pine and wych-elm and quiet as
the Northern fog banks.

I look back on mae life, swirled in grey sheets and ask, why did
I dae this, instead o' something else? And what did I dae? And
why didnae I? An old man sitting on a rock once told me all
love passes and all thought is dust. Who'll remember me when
I'm long gone awa' now that Mary's gone away . . . Faded out
like Strome . . . Strome and me and Mary . . . Blather on,
Jamie, and you've nothing tae fear . . .

In hospital they were all afeared, slack mooths and gogglin'
eens. Mae ward was filled wi' fatales tae be wrapped, crated

and slipped oot the back. I'd been deid meat tae but I'd come back from the deid so that made me special. I'd been tae the other warl' they talk o' so it was natural fer them tae ask what happened when I deid? They were going that way soon themselves so mebbe I could give them a few pointers – tell them what tae expect, how tae act on the other side. So I told them, dinnae I, Mary? I told 'em.

I said I was laying there deid in the dark wi' a gleam o' ice and the stillness o' a dark sea and then a grain of wind rose tae force five and a figure suddenly stood there. Angel or devil makes nae matter, it was a shock. He grabs me by mae lapels and lifts me oop easy as winking and I used tae be a braw man. 'Name?' he yowls. 'Jamie Drummond. And who might you be?' I replied. 'I'm the Dark Angel, the Soul-Gatherer. You're wanted, Drummond!'

Och I'm nobody much but that's no reason to curl oop and die. So I oops tae that Angel and says 'Jesu' – ah, swearing can be a great send-off tae a conversation – 'Jesu, it's yer job tae grab all those who come here and take them tae God-knows-where but that dinnae gives yer the right tae yowl and frighten folk.' 'I'm supposed tae frighten folk,' says the Angel. 'Weel I dinnae ken it's right. You shouldnae behave like some snot-snouted official from our warl'. This is the other warl' isn't it? A better warl', a warl' o' truth and mercy. It's nae place fer yer bullying. If yer go on wi' it I'll take it straight tae the top.'

'Weel, now's yer chance,' the Angel says wi' a sneer, and I was in a hall o' licht wi' starnies reeking froth from the Judge of the Universe on His bricht throne and I saw the lions o' God go by. So I sang tae keep mae spirits oop. (*Singing.*) 'Some say the devil's deid The devil's deid, the devil's deid Some say the devil's deid And buried in Kirkcaldy.'

'Jamie Drummond, cringe and tremble,' yowls a voice o' thunder. 'Yer here tae be judged and punished.' 'Why should I cringe and tremble?' I replied, 'I'm a Strome man. I'm nae afeared o' anything oop here. Dae yer ken what it's like doon there on earth fer ordinary folk like us? It's nae Heaven. Working men and wummen dinnae sleep on canny clouds or flutter their soft wings and play harps all day. It's work, morning tae evening, working the cold seas, and the black clouds rolling in like boulders from the west and the braw wind cutting like knives and all the waves above us: "Man overboard! – there – there! Puir Laurie's gone tae the deep!" And the next day, cold and wet, and the next and the next. Wha' punishment could you fright me wi' the noo?'

God was silent, as always. He hadnae had much truck wi' men from Strome afore. But it never does tae underestimate the Lord. In the end He chose a fitting punishment for me. He snapped His fingers and I found meself sneezing and opening mae eens. I was alive again. He'd given me another life sentence. His justice is awesome and with mae Mary taken from me the punishment was even harder tae bear. Mary, Mary, mae feerie lass I'm aye thinking o' thee . . .

It was a guid story I told 'em how I came back from the deid. The sick and dying were comforted . . . saw many a wee smile on dry lips and dull eens became brighter. Mebbe it was no' sae terrible after all . . . no need tae be afeared . . . Jamie Drummond says there's nothing tae be afeared o', sae long as yer speak oop.

All lies, o' course. I couldnae remember a thing o' what happened between when I deid, sneezed and sat up again. One moment I was falling out o' the warl', the next sneezing mae way back in . . . I dinnae ken what was in between.

I couldnae tell the others that, could I, Mary? Sae I told them o' the Dark Angel and standing oop and speaking oot . . . thought it would gi' 'em some comfort tae ken a Strome man had been awa' there in the darkness and was no' afeared . . . Helped them but it doesnae help me . . . I saw no licht, or lions, no Angel or Lord tae give the word tae . . . keep blathering and blethering, Jamie . . . I'm chitterin' on the road, Mary, and the cold grips mae heart again . . . (*Faint sound of bagpipes.*) List . . . list . . . is that the rising sun or a piper coming from afar? . . . Make them play the auld tunes, Mary . . . *The Welcome Owre the Main* or *Auld Stuart's Back Again*. (*Singing.*) 'Dance tae yer daddy Ma bonnie wee lassie Dance tae yer daddy Mae bonny wee lamb An' ye'll get a fishie In a little dishie. Ye'll get a fishie, when mae ship comes hame.' . . . No more gaps in the heart, all caulked over. Keep blathering and blethering, Jamie . . . och but listen tae the pipes, Mary, the pipes . . . (*The sound of the bagpipes grows louder.*) Keep blathering and blethering . . . the moudiewort, the moudiewort, the mumpin beast . . . Guid morning, Mary . . . Guid morning . . . Blathering and blethering . . . Dinnae stop talking and you'll be fine.

BILLY AND ME

Loud entrance music.

Billy All right, let me answer your question.

Jennings I haven't asked a question.

Billy I'll answer it anyway. Yes, of course, that's my wife. Would I have a maid that ugly? I may be out of touch with the common man but, by God, I can still spot a common roach.

Jennings I was only going to tell you I just saw a man-eating shark in the zoo.

Billy That's nothing. I just saw a man-eating herring in the park. And what's so great about playing the piano by ear? My grandfather was always fiddling with his whiskers. No, no, in all due modesty I really don't deserve this award. But then I have woodworm and I don't deserve that either. So where are you? Look at Lake Placid – all that water and that's only the top.

Jennings Good.

Billy Your timing's off.

Jennings *My* timing's off! I've got three lines.

Billy Three, thirty-three or three hundred and thirty-three – that's very difficult to say without taking a breath – you're still slow. And if you're slow, I'm slow. We're a double act remember.

Jennings You're right. I'm depressed.

Billy We've had this conversation before.

Jennings We've had every conversation before. I know I'm often depressed, but today I've turned it up a notch or two. I looked out of the window this morning and saw a grey sky, grey walls, grey streets, grey coats and faces as worn as stones.

Billy Ladies and Gentlemen, meet Michael Jennings, the original black hole of fun. Take another pill, Mike. Speak to him, Major, you're his uncle.

Major Pull yourself together, Laddie. Shoulders back, feet together – fire!

Jennings I've got this feeling if I sold candles the sun would never set, if I sold coffins people would stop dying, and if it rained gold I'd be asleep under some roof.

Billy Sailing down the north face of the Eiger I've often asked myself how come I'm not on anybody's short-list. But I certainly admire the way you've refused to let success undermine your natural lugubriousness.

Jennings No jokes, I'm not in the mood.

Billy Impossible. I'm only here to make jokes. Take another pill, Ambrose.

Jennings All my life looking for something that wasn't dull and boring. When I was eleven I got bored with my parents. My mother played the piano at children's parties and took in lodgers, and my father liked watching his fingernails grow.

Billy We've heard it all before. Aunt Agnes, say something.

Aunt Agnes Don't be silly, Michael, your parents weren't boring.

Jennings All parents are boring. One hundred and ten on the Richter scale of boredom.

Aunt Agnes Your Uncle George wasn't boring. When he retired he re-wrote hundreds of books, giving them all happy endings. Thanks to him Romeo and Juliet didn't die, Othello and Desdemona patched up their differences, and the Three Sisters got to Moscow. Uncle George was a great humanitarian.

Uncle Pat And sure his wife went bald in a cupboard, didn't she?

Billy You tell him, Uncle Pat!

Uncle Pat O'Pat to you.

Jennings I don't care about Uncle George. I feel so dull I can't even entertain a doubt. I'll turn white and die.

Billy You sound like six volumes of Dostoevsky. You're always being invited to parties.

Jennings They want to see you. Nobody would invite me without you. I just stand around using up air.

Billy True, but don't forget some of my brilliance is due to you.

Jennings *Some* of it? All of it.

Billy All of it? Take another pill, Delilah.

Jennings Yes, all of it. There's nothing you say I don't say for you.

Billy Delusions of grandeur now, matey.

Jennings No delusions, we're the same you and me.

Billy Don't flatter yourself, Jeffrey. We're chalk and cheese, oil and vinegar, Cain and Abel. Anyone with a pair of ears can tell that. We're absolutely, totally, unutterably – God that's a hard word to say when you're playing a nose-flute – different. Hey, maybe we should do the act with you playing a nose-flute through your left nostril? Think you could cope?

Aunt Agnes No, please don't try it, Michael. You could do yourself an injury.

Jennings There's no way I'm going to do anything with a flute stuck up my hooter. We're two sides of the same coin, Billy, take my word.

Billy I'll take nothing from you without wearing rubber gloves. We're different. I'm me, you're you, and never the twain shall meet.

Jennings I'm me *and* you.

Billy Take another pill, Alonso. You're unstable.

Jennings Of course I'm unstable. Everybody knows I'm unstable.

Uncle Pat Sure he's unstable.

Major Send for the MO.

Aunt Agnes Poor boy.

Jennings But I still know what I know. I created you.

Billy You what?

Jennings Created you.

Billy The ego of the man! If you walked down Lovers' Lane you'd hold hands with yourself. You couldn't create buttered turnips.

Jennings No, but I created, Master Billy Benton.

Billy It's absurd. We're dealing with a fully fledged one-hundred-proof loony.

Jennings Why do I have to keep repeating it? I created you, dummy.

Billy That's a terrible thing to say. I'm really upset, Arthur.

Jennings Of course you're upset. I'm upset so you're upset. How many times do I have to tell you? You're as thick as two planks – in fact you are two planks!

Billy And that comes from a man with the IQ of a dead trout.

Aunt Agnes Now, now, boys.

Jennings No, this is between Billy and me. Don't anyone interrupt.

Billy Just when did this act of God take place?

Jennings When I was ill.

Billy When you were inside for your breakdown you mean. So that's when you created us is it? One fine day you said *BANG* . . . and there we were.

Jennings No, it took years. He-ah-oh, he-ah-oh, he-ah-oh, trying to speak clearly, ah-oh-he, ah-oh-he, ah-oh-he, exercising my mouth, he-who-he, he-who-he, he-who-he, and my face muscles, who-he, who-he, who-he. Every morning and evening in front of the mirror learning to pronounce every word distinctly without moving my lips. Zzzzzzz-zod-zod-zod. That's how your voice was born, Billy, out of my voice. It had to be vibrant and strong. Mmmmmmmmm-ooooooo-mmmmmmm, laaaaaaabaaaabambam-aaaa-mmmmm. Other exercises to strengthen the tongue, moving it around in circles in front of the teeth, biting it eight times and sticking it out six; saying words like 'she, train, town, talk, guess, next, test' and 'sack' at speed, over and over, under and over. Then bringing you to life with finger manipulation. Do you know there are five distinct movements of the lever to open your mouth to say 'Hello, how are you'? Of course you don't. It's my movements that give you life, make you Billy Benton, and you Aunt Agnes, and you Uncle O'Pat, and you Major. For every emotion there's a different movement, sometimes two or three. When you laugh, Billy, I have to move the headstick back and forward. When you're surprised I open your mouth and move your body backwards. You can go from surprise to laughter, and back again in seconds. All the movements have to be that fast. Bolts of lightning put life into Frankenstein's Monster, with you it was sweat. My sweat made Billy Benton and the rest of the family.

Billy You've reduced Aunt Agnes and the others to silence.

Jennings I have to for the time being.

Billy Are you saying I'm just a ventriloquist's dummy?

Jennings Yes, yes, yes!

Billy But I feel real enough.

Jennings Say 'Little Billy Benton is only a dummy'.

Billy Little Billy Benton is only a dummy, little Billy Benton is only a dummy, little Billy Benton is only a dummy.

Jennings There you are.

Billy Why me? I'm just an inoffensive little fellow. Never done anyone any harm and then I have this pie thrown in my face. It's a bit of a let down and it's not worthy of you, Gregory.

Jennings But it's true.

Billy That's no excuse. Where would we all be if everyone went around telling the truth? It's horrible. This world's run on lies. Without lies we'd all be stripped bum-naked. Who could bear it? I think I speak for everyone here when I say who wants to know they're blocks of wood? Agnes doesn't nor does the Major and certainly not Uncle O'Pat who's heard too many thick Irishman jokes already. How would you like it if some old guy with a long white beard came down and said 'Sebastian Jennings, you're nothing, you don't exist, it's all me. My hand stuck up your back controlling every action you make from the time you open eyes – that's me – of a morning, till you close them – that's me too – at night. You've no thoughts or feelings of your own, everything's me.' I mean, Carlotta, that doesn't exactly encourage personal initiative does it? Pulls the rug right out from under. You'd ask yourself 'Why bother? I've no will of my own so what's the use?' It's particularly bad for someone like me who needs his own space. I'm just on the point of maturing like good wine. But every time I try to branch out, take my own road, you fill me with stuff like the truth, just to pull me down. It's cruel, Gerald. And I'm easily hurt. You don't think of me – ever.

Jennings It's not true. When we went on that tour of Israel didn't I remember to pack a pencil sharpener for you?

Billy That's a good joke – dirty, but good. But I'm in no mood for jokes. That tells you how upset I am.

Jennings I'm sorry, Billy, but I had to do it. The more independent you get, the duller I seem. All my natural wit and exuberance goes into you. I only get invited to funerals.

Billy But according to you I'm you anyway, so what's the problem?

Jennings Psychological. The fact you're becoming more independent is a sure sign I'm becoming more schizophrenic.

Billy OK. But it's great for the act.

Jennings There are other things beside the act.

Billy Not for me, Gotlieb.

Jennings No, I guess not. What a sham identity is. I used to stand for hours in front of a mirror in Jameson Psychiatric Wing looking at myself, not believing it. No link with me and the me staring back at me.

Billy Bad times. What with your voices and all.

Jennings They were going on in all directions, babbling one after the other, accusations and insinuations every twenty seconds. I was turned upside down. The voices knew things I didn't seem to know. Voices outside of me mocking in every corner, attacking from all sides.

Billy Yes and you could've gone around like the rest of them, listening and mumbling to yourself, 'You're a liar . . . I don't believe that . . . Never . . . No I didn't . . . It's all tittle-tattle . . .', talking to shop windows, trees and Number 10 buses. But you didn't. Instead you made your voices visible, made them work for you. You created Billy Benton and family, live flesh and blood or a reasonable facsimile. Isn't that right, Major?

Major Absolutely. Stout fella, Captain Jennings, didn't panic 'cept in a crisis. Fought the good fight. British grit. Came through with flying colours. Hip-hip.

Billy You'd agree with that wouldn't you, Uncle O'Pat?

Uncle Pat Why, sure, O'Billy. Michael here didn't go around casting his eyes ta heaven like a cat in a thunderstorm. God sent us ta Hell but He can't make us holler. I've got a tongue soft as a feather mattress but I'm here ta tell you we're all proud of you, lad.

Aunt Agnes You remember how we used to go around always accusing you of this and that, Michael. Nagging and complaining, always pointing out your faults, saying you cheated at cards, mugged old ladies, committed rape and murder and never took a bath. We don't say that now, dear, because you're a credit to us and yourself.

Jennings Thank you for your vote of confidence.

Billy I don't know why you need it. Top of the bill at Scarborough last summer and a TV series in the offing. What more do you want?

Jennings I'm still sick. The fact I'm talking with myself like this proves it.

Billy You're talking with Aunt Agnes and the family.

Jennings Same thing.

Billy You've done a lot despite your handicap – no, *because* of your handicap. You're an example to the rest. Mentals have their champions too you know.

Aunt Agnes Look at Miss Rosemary Miller, the catatonic who became a top artists' model. She could stand around for hours not moving a muscle – splendid person. Made a fortune.

Uncle Pat And what about Jack Flynn? So retarded he didn't qualify as a mental defective – leader writer for a Sunday newspaper isn't he? And proud of it.

Major And don't forget Harold Parker. You remember Harold from Fergerson Wing. Acute paranoid with homicidal tendencies. Left and got a job in MI5. Welcomed with open arms. No knowing how far he'll rise. And he's got work for at least five other inmates from the locked ward. Splendid chappie.

Uncle Pat You've joined those heroic ranks, Michael lad. They'll raise statues of you by the Liffey, blue plaques on houses you've never lived in.

Billy You've made ventriloquism do for schizophrenia what MI5 has done for paranoia.

Jennings I'd like to do more.

Billy You've done enough.

Jennings No, no, you've set me thinking. I've helped myself to overcome sickness of soul and mind, now I should try and help others.

Aunt Agnes Michael, you're not going to become a social worker are you?!

Major Shoot me somebody! For God's sake make somebody shoot me!

Jennings No, I was thinking of setting up classes for schizophrenics. It'll be occupational therapy at its best. Instead of art, music and group discussion they can have ventriloquism classes. Rows of schizophrenics sitting with little dummies on their knees practising: he-ah-oh, he-oh-oh, he-who, who-he, laaaabambambam-aaa-mmm and the tongues clicking and the little wooden head going up down all at once. Aside from the good it'll do for the patients, we could end up with enough speaking dummies to form an acting company – we could put on *Hamlet* or form a choir. A choir of dummies singing *The Messiah* or the *Hallelujah Chorus*.

Billy I've always wanted to sing Brunnehilde's farewell to Siegfried.

Jennings It could really catch on. We could even play the Albert Hall.

Aunt Agnes That would be nice, dear. You sound really enthusiastic.

Jennings I am. I feel much better now.

Uncle Pat That's grand, laddie, I think we should sing *Happy Days Are Here Again*.

Jennings Not all at once. I can't cope with more than one voice at a time.

Billy You see, talking it out with your family helped. That's why I got so upset when you said I was nothing more than a ventriloquist's dummy. All right, I'll concede I might've been that at the start. But nothing stays the same. Even ventriloquists' dummies evolve, mature, blossom. Let's face it, I've become more than just a block of wood and a voice. I'm a personality in my own right.

Aunt Agnes I think we've all grown a little.

Billy But me more than anyone. After all the show is called 'Billy and Me'! That's why I know I exist. I know! I've got thoughts, feelings. Mine, not yours. Thoughts, feelings, responsibilities. One of which is to see the act is in good shape for tonight's show. You've had your temperamental fit for today, Roger. Now we've got some practising to do. After all, you may be a schizophrenic but you're still a pro.

Jennings Always.

Major Straight down the line.

Billy We all are. So let's pick it up from where we left off . . . My reason for wanting to join the Metropolitan Police, ladies and gentlemen, is because I care deeply about the national decline in personal standards, and the corresponding growth of greed and selfishness, plus I like the uniform, the money, the perks, and the unlimited power to bash anyone I want to.

Jennings Yes, but why do you call your dog Blacksmith?

Billy I call him Blacksmith because every time I open the door he makes a bolt for it . . .

Loud exit music.

LOSING MYSELF

Adams There's rain in the air, Maurice. Look at the smoke
from the pile of burning leaves and the sun going down behind
the row of gravestones. Have you noticed death is all in rows?
Alive or dead you have to stay in line. Alive or dead it's much
the same. You understand, Maurice. That's why I've taken to
saying 'Hello' to you most evenings. Nowadays I don't say
'Hello' to many people. Silence is good for the wise and even
better for idiots. On the other hand, talking lightens the load a
little and misery loves company.

I liked the sound of you from the start. 'Here lies Maurice
Becker. Gentleman of Heart and Soul. Born July 29th, 1882.
Died August 1950. Alone.' That last word 'Alone' made me
want to sit and talk. You weren't afraid to say you died alone.
All the other gravestones read as though the dead went
surrounded by friends or loved ones. Wishful thinking, whistling
in the dark, Maurice.

But you're going to be alone now, friend. Left for dead. You
and me both. I haven't told you before, hoping something might
turn up. But it hasn't and it won't. The truth is, Cramer Street
Cemetery is closing down by order of the Council. Tomorrow
morning the shutters go up and the bulldozers move in. All
legal and official. We've lost this one. They've got round the
little problem of building on a disused burial ground so you'll
soon be lying under concrete instead of earth – weeds between
the paving stones – and I'll be on the drift between here and
nowhere.

Land's too expensive to house the dead nowadays, Maurice. We
can't afford to let you and the others rest in six feet of it, free.
Not when there's money to be made. It was obvious what was
going to happen. This has been a disused burial ground for
some time now and the staff were gradually moved out until
there was only me left, half-mad and long past it. Just look at
the place, Maurice, weeds and flowers and ragged walks. You
wouldn't call it a well-run cemetery except for foxes and
badgers. It smells of decay like tropical fruit on the wind. I've

done my best but I was trained in medicine not burial maintenance so the tombs crumble, the stone lilies crack and moss creeps over everything.

That's how they planned it I suppose. They neglect a property, let it fall into ruins, then knock it down during the night because it's no longer safe. They pitch you out of doors, sonny, neck and heels, before Christmas. You wouldn't know about such tricks, Maurice. It's not a gentleman's world now. As for heart and soul – what are they?

This cemetery's easy picking for speculators. It's never been fashionable. How could it be with a railway yard on one side, an empty slaughterhouse on the other and piles of rubbish smouldering on the far shore. There's never been anyone to stand up for it, alive or dead. Highgate Cemetery's lucky with Marx, the Rossettis and Charles Cruft of the Dog Show Crufts, buried there. It means you've got intellectuals, romantics and dog-lovers in your corner. Not many politicians would care to go up against that lot. We're not in that league. We haven't even got a decent criminal in residence like Hampstead Cemetery with Jenny Diver.

Of course the famous dead won't save Highgate or Hampstead cemeteries forever. They'll all go under. Nothing'll save them. Piety can never hold out against profit. Soon it'll be burning all along the line; crematoriums, world wide. 'Next time the fire.' That's what it means, Maurice. Fires, fires, everlasting fires – so say 'Good night'. Too many people dying and the earth isn't big enough to house them all in bulk. They have to be reduced to manageable proportions so instead of rows of headstones, there'll be rows of chimneys: black smoke and crows filling the sky.

Demolitions have already started on the west side, Maurice, along Usher Road. The poor get it first even in death. That's where the bone-pits are. Dozens of them packed with poor bones, skulls, tibias and other spare parts. In the old days the poor used to rent graves. They couldn't afford to buy a plot outright, so they'd rent one for five or ten years. When their time was up, out they'd come and into the bone-pits with 'em. Then the empty grave was rented to somebody else. There's thrift and profit there, Maurice. True as the needle to the pole, it's what makes the world go round. No appeal.

Don't you find death like life, Maurice? On the one side we've got expensive resting places, on the other, the poor are piled up in heaps like so much rubbish. Yet they're the same thing – bones. Like you are now, friend. There's respect for bones here, but none over there where they couldn't pay for it. Where's the logic? Either bones are something to respect, in which case don't fling them into pits, or they're nothing and the dead are somewhere else. In which case why bother with tombs, flowers, bare heads, and silences? Just as well sing psalms to a dead horse.

Have you heard the story of the man who spent a night in one of the Cramer Road bone-pits for a bet? When he came out next morning he was just the same as he went in – dull as dishwater. No imagination, Maurice. He was the same the next day and the next. On the third day he stopped talking. On the fourth he lost control of his mind. On the fifth, he went mad.

You could tell us about bones, Maurice, if bones could speak. Perhaps there is something in them, something left over from the life they led and the flesh they supported. In which case mine will be troubled. This is probably our last talk together, Maurice, so I should tell you about myself. I haven't done it before. There must've been dozens of questions you wanted to ask but never did. You are a gentleman, Maurice, you never pried. You've been as silent as the shades of death.

I'm frightened, Maurice, dead eyes in doorways. What am I going to do outside with the living? I don't fancy it. If you've got religious beliefs it's different. What does present misery matter beside eternity in Paradise? You have to have rock-like faith to confront life. But we know the true truth of it. This universe came out of a chaos that always was and will go back to a chaos that always will be; a universe with no edge to it, no space to it, no beginning or end to it and with nothing for a Creator to do in it, even if he or she wanted to. And so despair creeps in and you're lost.

I used to have faith, Maurice, but I lost it. I was always losing things; gloves, keys, money, hope and a rocking-horse called

Bill. It's as if they were spirited away. Something out there was always taking things that were mine. How did I come to lose that rocking-horse for example? And hope. Rocking-horses and hopes don't just disappear down rabbit holes. They were too big for that, so where did they go? Who stole them? That's what I want to know. There's a thief out there and he's never been caught.

Of course losing things so early on taught me not to get too attached to anything. I was sure to lose it.

Perhaps that's why I fell in love when I was studying medicine. She was an anarchist from the London School of Economics – sweep away the tyrants and then something wonderful would happen. Ah yes, yes indeed . . .

We lived together and even had a child together. But then one evening I just turned around and she wasn't there. I thought maybe she'd gone out for cigarettes or been kidnapped by gypsies. No, I'd just lost her. She'd long gone with an old friend of mine and I hadn't noticed. Later she married a scrap-metal merchant from Poole and ended up running a vegetarian restaurant in Norfolk. Property is theft and reality hangs by a thread, Maurice.

She left me with our child, Emma. Emma after Emma Goldman. Beautiful girl but my time with her was soon up. She found herself a stockbroker and that was that. We lost touch. That's something else I lost – touch. I'm even going to lose touch with you, Maurice, and you're dead.

Dust and shredded memories . . . spider-webs . . . pale word-dust falling from my mind. Boys on roller-skates turning slow circles in empty streets . . . My father wanting me to go into the Church. I was always reading the Bible. But then I started asking questions. Could God kill and torture innocent children and not be a murderer? And if God could have a son why not a daughter? I marked passage after passage in the book that puzzled me but I never got an answer to any of my questions. I lost my faith before I lost my virginity and I didn't miss either.

Instead of going into the Church I went into medicine. I was

young, I wore my heart on my sleeve. I believed in serving
humanity. Widows and orphans, the poor, sick and oppressed
were my patients. I was on the right side from the start.
Though of course widows can be cruel and orphans wicked.
Though we don't talk about that.

Every morning I'd go into my surgery in the Isle of Dogs and
see the tired bones and worn faces, coughing and spitting up
their heart's blood. So many bodies and minds blunted from
birth. I'd prescribe soothing words as well as medicines. I don't
know if I helped but they were always grateful. 'Thank you,
Doctor, for saving my boy . . . my wife . . . me!' I'm sure you'd
be grateful too if you thought I'd been able to save you,
wouldn't you, Maurice?

I became successful. Now I'm as poor as a winter crow but then
I was successful. I opened a surgery in Harley Street. No, I
didn't neglect my Dogs' practice. Far from it. I used my
influence to get hospital and Day-Care Centres built where they
were needed. I didn't do it for money or recognition. In fact I
rejected rewards of any kind when I was offered them. People
knew that and I was admired as a true, caring human being. I
became something of a legend.

Did you ever think about suicide, Maurice? Doctors do. They
touch death so often it holds few terrors for them. And, of
course, we have easy access to drugs and other potions. We can
mix a soft and easy death for ourselves. As others have pointed
out, there is a problem about suicide. It never works the way it
should. What does? Most people commit suicide in order to get
themselves taken seriously. That's the important thing – to be
taken seriously. So long as you're alive other people never seem
convinced by what you do or what you say. But if you've killed
yourself you're suddenly very convincing. You're taken seriously
at last. Unfortunately you aren't around to enjoy the triumph.

I was never tempted to try it but one night I was crossing a
bridge on my way home when I heard footsteps behind me.
There was a faint cough and a fainter splash, Icarus had fallen
from the sky far, far away in the background of the picture. Or
had he – or she – or even them? When I turned back the bridge
was deserted. I looked down over the parapet. Was there

someone way below in the water? I don't know, it was so dark. Anyway I didn't try to find out. I wasn't going to get wet. I didn't even report the incident. Actually I forgot. I find it easy to forget things.

I don't think anyone jumped. It was all a trick of the night. But even if they had, what was that to me? The truth was, despite all my good works, I never believed there was anything serious enough in the world to care about. How could anyone work themselves up over money, fame, ideals, love or death? What was so important about them?

The one real pleasure I had in life was the thought of my own worth. Unfortunately after that incident – real or imagined – I lost the ability to fool myself. That's another loss there. Are you keeping count, Maurice? I saw my concern for others was pure condescension. We all have to find people who are even less than ourselves and there are none easier to lord it over than the poor, the sick and the dying. They were the least and I was the most. As a dedicated doctor I always had the last word. That's the important thing, not the first but the last word.

Now words fall from my mind, Maurice. My father told me if you can't be good, act it, because if you act something you are it. I tried. Oh, how I tried. I acted the caring man but the caring wasn't there and never came. I lost my way.

I've often thought of the man or woman who drowned – if anyone did drown that is. I'm sure they didn't. But if they did it would've been good if they could've tried to drown themselves again. That way I'd've had a second chance to save them. I crossed that bridge scores of times after but there was no more jumping. Just as well perhaps. On second thought I was lucky to be spared a second chance. Like everyone else I'd've done the same thing all over again – nothing. I wouldn't have changed and the guilt would have been doubled.

It's going to rain, Maurice. Do you ever hear footsteps behind you? No, of course you don't. How could you? I hear them at night, when I'm trying to sleep. Footsteps going away from me not coming towards me. Very faint. Some people hear voices, laughter in the night. I hear footsteps.

I had money, power and a wide circle of friends. My health was good and I slept well and rarely alone. And I walked away from it all like those footsteps. I lost heart. That's the worst loss of all. All other losses are nothing to that loss. Slowly my body melted from inside, flesh and bones turning to jelly. Another body floated half-in and half-out of this body. I lost the sense of my body's outline. I didn't know where my limbs were or my head. I wasn't there. Or here. Or anywhere . . .

It starts to rain.

I wore out like an old steam-engine and just tumbled to pieces simultaneously. Friends couldn't understand why I judged myself and found myself so guilty. They were like me and didn't feel guilty. It seemed they had guessed my compassion for the poor was only a mask. They applauded it, thought it a very neat trick. After all, true goodness rarely makes its owner attractive. But I couldn't stop judging myself. There were no good intentions, no extenuating circumstances. I couldn't live with myself or with other people, knowing that they were like me.

Time is only what keeps everything from happening at once and nature has no destination; chance holds the reins. It's all action without cause or reason. We invent causes and reasons so as not to be afraid.

Alcohol saw me through but I could never get enough of it. It rots more than the liver, Maurice, memory-bubbles bursting in the brain. I stopped practising medicine and drifted here to tend the dead not the living. I'd lost myself. That's the last loss, before the final loss.

It's raining hard now, Maurice. Perhaps it rained like this on the first day of the great deluge when God sent pure water to wash away the world's sins, my sins. No, it couldn't wash away mine let alone the world's, they are too dark. Water makes the desert bloom, the green carpet spread, purifies the stones but not our hearts. Not mine, not theirs.

The rain falls with increasing force.

Will this rain wash away your grave and me, Maurice? The greatest service you can do for a god is to drown. For then you return to the first element, the Deep, the Deep, from which all things flow and are born again. And so the Lord opened seven floodgates of Heaven and the mouths of the fountains and the floodgates began to pour down water from Heaven and the fountains of the Deep sent up waters until the whole world was full of water and washed clean, clean, again! . . .

The rain pours down drowning out all other sounds.

HOUDINI'S HEIR

Jackson Houdini escaped from milk-cans, trunks, barrels, coffins, blocks of ice, car-tyres, glass tubes, cabinets, valises and strait-jackets, suspended head down from cranes eighty feet up. There's no call for such stuff now. Escapology as an art-form is deader than dead mutton. You lot standing there like so many tired vultures scared out of a year's growth don't want to see anyone throw off the chains that bind them. You'd like everyone to stay locked and padlocked. It's more comfortable that way. You get no joy out of seeing a man like me bursting free against the odds.

I'm in the great tradition. Henry 'Escape' Jackson's the name, the one and only, Houdini's heir, the last of his kind. That's why I'm standing here in early autumn, stripped to the waist, outside the Tower of London, trying to entertain the likes of you. In the good times Houdini called himself an expert in extrication and self-release but I'm just busking for my bread and it's hard pickings I can tell you. I'm the only one left carrying the torch. No more pure Houdinis left except me.

This afternoon I'm not going to escape suspended from the Bloody Tower in a steel box. You wouldn't appreciate it and the authorities wouldn't allow it. They don't want to encourage escapes of any kind. It sets a bad example. The world's a prison and people are either inmates or warders and it doesn't sit well with the warders if someone goes around showing how easy prisons can be broken out of. That's why I've always had problems. So many obstacles and I never reached my potential. Of course a freed man isn't a free man – but we can all still escape if we want to. Most of you don't even try!

Though you don't deserve it I'm going to show you how to escape from a strait-jacket, chains and handcuffs. And not from behind a curtain or trick cabinet either, where keys and other tools can be hidden. Houdini used to tape them onto the soles of his feet – knives, files, extensions, wires, picks, he had 'em stuck up every orifice he could find. Houdini was the best.

I work in full view of my audience. I've nothing to hide. It's all done by diabolical dexterity and superhuman muscular control. It's a matter of skill and fitness. There's no one fitter for his age than me, south of Watford . . . (*He slaps his stomach.*) Stomach rock-hard. Just feel . . . (*He slaps his stomach again.*) No, on second thoughts, I don't want any of you poking away at me. Who knows where your fingers've been?

Mine is a classic act of escapology, ladies and gentlemen, without a single gimmick. Except one. During my act, when my arms never leave my body, I talk – about anything and everything. I have other interests besides escapology. Hypnotism for example. I think it might be a cure for AIDS if only they could find it. Talk is what makes 'Escape' Jackson unique. I talk about myself mostly, tell stories, jokes, even a sermon or two. My last one, 'The Meek Shall Inherit The Earth', had them rolling in the aisles. I've known it all, drunk the sparkle and the foam, the gall and the wormwood, and I'm still trying. Fascinating stuff to listen to and if you don't listen I'll turn you over to the police. They'll know what to do.

You laymen won't understand just how difficult it is to talk and escape at the same time. Even the great Houdini asked for complete silence during his act so he could concentrate. But I've trained myself so I can talk and escape both – and if you listen closely you can also hear the sound of one hand clapping.

Now my assistant Mr George Kelly will pass amongst you with the chains, cuffs, and strait-jacket so you can examine them . . . (**George** *picks up the implements and moves about with them.*) You'll see they are just standard equipment found in any police-station and lunatic asylum. Most of you will be familiar with them. Oh no, you don't fool me, not for a minute! You've had 'em on. If you stay here you'll find out how to get 'em off the next time you're caught.

You'll see the chains and the rest of the stuff hasn't been tampered with. Houdini escaped from a Bonza strait-jacket, mid-air, Nottingham, January 12th, 1911 by hiding a blade in the sleeves to cut the straps. But there's nothing up my sleeve. Look . . . Go on, look . . . look . . . it won't bite you.

Right, that's enough, George . . . (**George** *brings back the
equipment and drops it on the ground.*) I usually disinfect everything
after it's been handled by the public but I'll take a chance
today and work with dirty tools.

George, the strait-jacket first if you please . . . (**George** *puts
the strait-jacket on him.*) I put my arms into the sleeves . . . Now,
George will do up the straps and buckles. But I don't really
need to explain do I? You're crackers the lot of you. I'm
the only sane one here, though I've often seen the swallow in
tomorrow's sky. But I know what you're asking. If I'm the only
sane one, why am I the only one in a strait-jacket? That's easy.
If they tried to restrain all the crazies around here they'd run
out of jackets. It's easier to strait-jacket the single sane man.
Remember that the next time you visit mentals . . . Tighter,
George . . . Good . . . good . . . I ask myself why am I standing
here, shivering in a strait-jacket with a cold wind blowing up
my right trouser-leg? The reason is, God drops parcels from
Heaven for every human being on earth and some get packages
filled with good things whilst others get bundles filled with
trouble. Now when God threw down my bundle He hit me
straight on the noggin with it – bang! Accident, of course, but it
knocked me witless. Otherwise I wouldn't be here having to
show my art to the likes of you . . . Tighter, George . . . pull the
straps tighter, *ahhh* . . . That's it . . . You can't escape from
strait-jackets by brute force . . . you have to be subtle to get
them off.

The first place I escaped from was Bardsley Home for Boys,
Northampton. I was sent there when I was twelve. My Mum
and Dad had just scarpered and my grandfather was dying.
That's something no one can escape from, not even Houdini.
Starved himself to death because he thought the doctors were
poisoning him. My grandmother had a bone stuck in her throat
for years and they couldn't ever find it. There's something
funny there. One breakfast I left fat on my plate. I hate fatty
bacon. The Matron, who used to wear a mohair wig and
home-made eyebrows, told me to eat it up. I wouldn't and she
locked me in the bedroom but I picked the lock and was up, off
and away.

I changed my name like Houdini. That's why we've got so

much in common. It's what makes us so close. My mother was Irish. I'm a distant relative of the famous American footballer 'Wrong Way' Harrigan who ran the length of the pitch to score for the wrong side. My father was a Root. I couldn't call myself 'Escape' Root could I? So I changed it. Hard decision. I'm proud of being a Root. We have a great history in Northampton.

When the hell-fire preacher Jonathan Edwards discovered some children reading a book for midwives and had a committee set up to punish them it was a Root – young Timothy Root – who outfaced the whole pack of 'em. Edwards, the committee, the town dignitaries – the lot. He told 'em, 'You are nothing but men, moulded up of a little dirt, and I don't care a turd. I don't give a fart for any of you.' That's a true Root for you.

And talking of farts. I never fart. That's something you shouldn't let escape. No need, if you learn to control your body and squeeze your bum tighter. It'll save you ladies getting bubbles down your tights or you gentlemen having to put your trousers down inside your socks.

That's enough of the strait-jacket, George. Straps and buckles all secure . . . see, can't move my arms . . . *ahh* . . . *ahh* . . . (*He strains to move his arms.*) In the old days, 1914, New York Hippodrome, Houdini appeared in a strait-jacket with Eva Tanguay, Eddie Foy, and six marines. No, they weren't all in the same strait-jacket. They just helped lace him into one. Now I have to be content with George here. That's how far downhill it's all gone . . . Right, George, the handcuffs, if you please. They're standard issue. Not like the Big Bean Monster cuffs invented by Captain Bean of Boston, 1910. They were supposed to be impregnable but Houdini got out of 'em in six minutes flat. What a man! Brothers under the skin. Snap 'em on, sonny . . . (*The handcuffs are snapped on.*) Now will someone in the audience examine 'em? Don't be shy. Oh, very well, I'll hop over to you and make it easier . . . (*He hops forward.*) You, madam . . . pull . . . the handcuffs . . . pull the handcuffs . . . that's it! Good . . . satisfied? . . . (*He hops back.*) Now for the chains . . . George, the chains . . . (**George** *picks up the chains.*) My assistant will now bind me securely with the chains whilst I keep talking . . . (**George** *begins to slowly wind the*

chains round him.) I haven't always been a professional
escapologist. I did other jobs – Monday to Friday dying –
labourer, food-packer, spot-welder in a car plant. Eight hours a
day, 3.30 p.m. to midnight. A hundred production lines going
full blast so you couldn't speak, the sparks would fill your
mouth. All you could do was work and dream of escaping.

The truth is I wasn't much good at anything till I found my
vocation. They said I couldn't organise a piss-up in a brewery.
One day I did. I arranged a party at Charrington Brewery,
Aldgate, but somehow I put the wrong day on the notice-board
and everyone turned up forty-eight hours early. I couldn't drive
a car either. I got nine traffic tickets in twenty minutes before I
discovered I was driving on the wrong side of the road.
Sometimes I used to feel like a man boiling his watch and
holding an egg in his hand to time it.

But I knew that wasn't the real me. My destiny was to play
summer seasons at Blackpool and close the first half of the bill
at Skegness. 'Escape' Jackson was to become a name . . . Wrap
it tight round the thighs, George . . . *ahh* . . . careful, lad, or
you'll be making me sing in a higher key.

I assisted William le Roy, 'The Nail King', who could take a
nail in his teeth and push it through a one-inch plank, and the
Great Marco who swallowed fifteen frogs, live . . . The arms,
George, don't forget the arms! . . . You should've seen Betty
Goodchild on tippy-toe on the back of a horse . . . wild as a
fawn, sweet as maple sugar, what a picture. She didn't take me
seriously till she saw me standing on Clifton Suspension Bridge,
hands and feet cuffed. I thought I'd impress her y'see . . . I said
I loved her and jumped . . . That's enough, George . . . Now
the final touch – the padlocks . . . (**George** *picks up the padlocks.*)
I hit the water and got rid of the leg irons. They'd been fixed
beforehand. But to open the handcuffs I had to bang them
against a piece of metal I'd strapped to my waist – an old
Houdini trick that's not so easy under water . . . *bang* . . . *bang*
. . . no good . . . I came up for air then went under again . . .
(**George** *puts the first padlock round the chains.*) Bang . . . bang . . . I
finally got rid of the handcuffs . . . I surfaced and waved.
Then I realised I'd forgotten something very important – I
couldn't swim . . . (*The second padlock is put on.*) I thought I was

played out, a trumped Jack, but some fisherman saw me thrashing about and pulled me in. That was a lucky escape. But it was more than luck, it was my destiny.

Betty and me got married. I turned up at the wedding in a top hat. How do you get a man my size into a top hat? You'll have to ask the Magic Circle. My lips are sealed. Betty and me set up home together but you get tired even of sugared almonds . . . I escaped, up, off and away . . . (*A third padlock is put on the chains.*) That's it, George . . . You see, ladies and gentlemen, I can't move a muscle. Trussed up like a mummy. Hog-tied tight. Now watch me do the impossible and burst free.

But first, George will pass amongst you with the collection plate. I appeal to your generosity, ladies and gentlemen, I've got expenses and you won't see the like of me ever again . . . They'd like to get me into a hostel but I'm not turning up at no turnstile every Monday for my fifty-pence pocket money and have to say 'Thank you'. When you reach my age God lowers a rope from Heaven down into the room where you're sleeping and it curls itself round your neck and hauls you up – unless Elijah cuts it for you. I don't need no Elijah. I'm an escape artist, I do my own cutting.

While the money's rolling in I'll give you a taste of my extraordinary powers . . . starting with the padlocks . . . (*There are repeated gasps and strained grunts as he tries to shake off the padlocks.*) Houdini was the greatest . . . got himself arrested and escaped from jails all over the world . . . great publicity . . . I tried it but they kept re-arresting me . . . I spent years inside that way . . . ahh . . . ahhhhh . . . (*A padlock drops onto the ground.*) There! . . . First padlock down . . . (*He continues straining.*) Houdini probed the mysteries of the Universe . . . had his ear cocked to the sounds of fraud from outer space . . . asked questions . . . like who was Adam? . . . Why are eggs shaped like that? . . . He escaped the confines of this world . . . ahhhh . . . (*The second padlock drops.*) Lock number two off and away! . . . (*He continues grunting and straining.*) Strength and endurance . . . cunning . . . knowing how and when . . . and what and why? . . . ahh . . . arrgghh . . . (*The third padlock drops to the ground.*) Three padlocks gone! . . . Well, don't just stand there – applaud! . . . (*There is a spattering of applause.*) You're a

hard audience. I just hope you're a sight more generous with
your money . . . Now the chains . . . This is more difficult . . .
tricky things chains . . . First I jump on the spot . . . Up and
down . . . up and down . . . (*He jumps energetically up and down.*)
Not . . . very . . . dignified . . . But . . . never been that . . .
Now I have to get into a prone position . . . flat on the ground
. . . only one way . . . have to go over . . . so . . . I sway back
and forward . . . back and forward . . . *ahh eeeeee* . . . (*He crashes
to the ground: a pause.*) Where am I? What happened? . . . Oh yes
. . . I have to wriggle and roll. This is a hernia potential act all
right. Stay clear when I'm rolling . . . (*There is a great clatter as he
rolls about.*) Stay clear! You'll get your toes crushed . . . Different
in Houdini's day . . . Audiences packed theatres . . . even if
they didn't actually see him escape . . . He'd be chained up like
this . . . put in a trunk or something and they'd stare at it for
maybe an hour before he'd suddenly jump out free . . . *urrghh.*
They never saw him actually escape . . . just stared at the box
he was in . . . nobody left . . . like some of you want to do now
. . . I can see even if I am on the ground . . . You'd prefer
snooker wouldn't you, it's quicker . . . before you know it two
minutes have flown past . . . *ooch* . . . who left all this litter
strewn about? . . . Bloody beer cans . . . say no to grubbiness,
fight filth! . . . Nowadays public squalor doesn't matter 'cause
anyone can be rich if they have the money . . . *ahhh* . . . *ooohh*
. . . George, why didn't you clear the bloody ground?! . . . I'm a
fatalist . . . nobody escapes their fate not even Houdini . . .
punched in the stomach . . . ruptured . . . died . . . *eeeh* . . . You
eat an apple *ahh* . . . kick a stone *eerk* . . . sneeze and see a
sparrow fall *ooohh* . . . It's ordained . . . everything we do . . .
even this . . . written . . . in the Book . . . no commentary so
nobody knows what the hell it all means . . . no story . . . just
lots of things happening because they happen . . . you can't
escape it . . . though you have to try . . . like me . . . (*He is
panting hard.*) I keep trying . . . Jesu, George, you've tied this too
tight today . . . no sweat . . . I'll get 'em off . . . Houdini never
gave up . . . Keep trying . . . George . . . George? Where are
you . . . George! . . . Anyone seen my assistant?! . . . George! . .
. My God, he's gone! . . . The little bastard's gone! . . . The
money? . . . Where's the money? . . . He's taken the collection!
Thief! . . . Thief! . . . Never trust an Irishman in green

shoes! . . . It's all right, I'll get the sod! . . . Houdini said . . .
just a matter of time and you can escape from anything . . .
arrhh arrhh . . . Don't go! . . . I can see you sidling off . . . Just
'cause there's a few spots of rain . . . it's nothing . . . *urrrhh* . . .
ugggg . . . stay . . . *eerrrkkk* . . . *ug* . . . don't go . . . don't go . . .
ekkkk ahhh errrr . . .

*It begins to rain and we slowly fade out as, clanking and cursing, he
frantically strives to get free.*

A TRUE-BORN ENGLISHMAN

Bray Of course, I'm covered by the Official Secrets Act, but then who isn't? There are some even who have to get clearance to talk to themselves. We've so many things that have to be kept secret. Anyway, if people know your secrets they're stealing something from you aren't they? Keep your mouth shut is my motto. Better still ask somebody to keep it shut for you. That's the way we like it. We're a closed, closed-mouth society; always have been.

I'm employed at Buckingham Palace so naturally most of what I know is top secret but I got official permission for this talk. I wanted you to share, with me, the joy I've had out the last twenty-five years, serving our Queen. I could've sold my story twice over to the Press – all the tits and lies fit to print – but I've never been tempted. It's true we aren't overpaid at the Palace. We can earn more elsewhere but we prefer the Royal Household because of the social prestige involved. And to be fair, there are perks. Palace staff are allowed to go to the Royal Race Meeting at Ascot in June. We're given passes which allow us onto the roof of the Royal Stand where we get a wonderful view of the racing. We're also given passes to the grandstand and the paddock but not, of course, the Royal Enclosure. That's not for the likes of us. But every Christmas we assemble in the great ballroom and file slowly past the Queen and curtsey or bow, and we're given our presents – usually a small doily with the royal coat of arms. Precious mementoes. I've got dozens of them in my bottom drawer. I've often thought of putting them on display at some gallery or other. I'll bet thousands would pay good money to see them.

With perks like that it's no wonder we're never tempted away from the Palace by bigger salaries. I'm being paid nothing for this talk for example, even though as a Conservative I always feel there is something offensive about any transaction in which money does not change hands.

But after thirty years serving Her Majesty, I know where my duty lies. It is to uphold the dignity of the Crown at all times.

Most of us at the Palace feel the same way. Of course you sometimes get a bad apple even there. Just last year we had a problem with a young woman who had been taken on as a clerk to the Queen's Household. Her references turned out to be phoney. She didn't come from a county family but was really the daughter of a grocer. Frankly, I don't think she was English. A true Englishwoman would never jeopardise her chances of serving her superiors in that way. I don't want to talk politics but it's why it's right for us to change from a manufacturing economy to a service one. Everybody agrees we English make the best valets and maids; we know how to take orders. Just as I know things everybody else wants to know – that the Queen uses black blotting paper on her desk and actually pours her own coffee from a pot at breakfast and when she was young she taught President Eisenhower how to dance the eightsome reel. That's never come out before. The gutter press would've paid me thousands for that tit-bit but I'm giving it to you free. I'm like that.

You know, I still can't believe that plain Leslie Bray of 42a The Cedars, Plumstead, ended up at Buckingham Palace. At school, they all thought I'd be something very small and subordinate in life. Little did they know. My parents would've been proud. At least my mother would. She was from Sydenham; played the piano at children's parties and her cherry cake was famous. My father was on the music-halls. During the war he went on ENSA tours to brutalise the troops. Jack Bray, the Yorkshire Yodeller. That was before he changed his act and became Jocko O'Bray, coming on in black face and kilt and singing *Danny Boy*. He played the bottom half of the bill all his life. If only he could see me playing the Palace.

But I spent my childhood in that floating world. Nothing permanent there. Pretty terrifying really, never knowing which town you were in. My mother hated it. They broke up when the music-halls closed and my father started playing in working men's clubs. She told him outright. 'Load of Communists drinking beer at fivepence a pint. You can't work for Communists.' She was so Conservative, when she was old and gone, she thought of having her heart transplanted to her right to counteract the mistake made by the Creator.

Well, my connection with the Palace began one night when I was temporary porter at another Palace – The Palace Hotel, Paddington. Two stars and so seedy it was sprouting. I was on duty when the call came, 2nd April 10p.m. It was Charles Twiggs, a man I'd met a few weeks previous at the Plumstead Dinner and Dance. We became friends, though I didn't know much about him.

'Les,' he said, 'would you like a job at Buckingham Palace?' I choked on my stout and checked the date. It was the 2nd not the 1st of April. In any case Charles Twiggs was not into humour.

I couldn't sleep that night and I knew I wouldn't be able to throw a decent dart 'til it was all over. I never have been good at interviews. Earlier, I'd wanted to join the Metropolitan Police but I was so nervous before the first interview I took a couple of drinks or more to steady my nerves. The way I answered the questionnaire I don't think helped much. I filled in 'Age', 'Height', 'Colour of Eyes' correctly but under 'Sex' I wrote 'Yes please'.

I didn't want to make that kind of mistake again so next morning I turned up at Buckingham Palace stone cold sober. I told the policeman on duty I had an appointment. He looked on his list and waved me in. That's the only way to get on in this life – be on the right list and you can get in anywhere.

I was directed across the forecourt to the visitors' door on the right. A porter in a red and blue livery checked another list and took me down to the basement and along corridors past men and women carrying piles of sheets, tablecloths, dirty pots, half-eaten food. It was just like being backstage at the Palace Hotel: this was a large hotel too but with a very select clientele of eight people and three-quarters of the rooms always empty.

I was taken to see Sir John Hall, then Master of the Household, and his assistant George Oliver, Comptroller of Supply. 'Get your hair cut, Mr Bray,' were the first words Sir John said to me. 'This isn't the place for gypsies, bedouins or poets. Bray? Bray? Weren't you personal valet to Lord Dunderdale? Pink-Tights Dunderdale we used to call him.' 'No, but I was waiter at the Hotel de Paris.' I replied. They then asked if I was married. I said 'No'. I had been but she walked out on me with a tenor. When she heard I had this job at Buckingham Palace she wanted to come back. I kicked her out.

They asked a few more questions like if I had any hobbies and I told them I was into modelling. I was making a replica of the Great Wall of China out of toothpicks. What I didn't know was they were in the middle of a crisis. They had just lost a footman with DTs and they needed a replacement quickly as there was a State Banquet in a couple of days' time. As chief porter, Twiggs' word carried weight – I was given six months' trial and a uniform. I like wearing a uniform. It sets you apart from all those people walking around in dirty clothes. And at the same time you don't have to make a choice every morning what you're going to wear: you know.

So I was in. The Germans have schools for servants where they teach people the principles of service. We English don't need to be taught. It comes natural, something we drink in with our mother's milk. Part of being a true-born Englishman. Of course, even for naturals, it takes time to adapt to the rules and reach the required degree of servility. I made mistakes at first. I was far too enthusiastic. We English don't like that. And then, worse, I had ideas. They aren't encouraged at the Palace, or anywhere else for that matter. Once, early on, I plucked up courage to see the Comptroller of Supply with this idea. Every morning for the last forty years the Royal Family have been served hot muffins wrapped in a warm napkin for breakfast. But they didn't like hot muffins; no one liked hot muffins. So every morning for forty years they were taken back into the kitchen and unwrapped. I suggested to the Comptroller it might be a good idea if we didn't serve hot muffins for breakfast.

He thought about it for a moment, then said 'Yes, that is a good idea, Bray. A very good idea. But around here we don't rush blindly into any blessed thing just because it happens to be a good idea.' You can always learn from your betters; lucky there are so many of them. I had to accept that tradition meant leaving things as they are. Change one thing and everything changes. And anyway ideas only come, if at all, from the top. When they came from the opposite direction it would be a signal for the end of our way of life. I found out early on, people with ideas end up living under a hedge without a penny-piece.

For a footman, obedience, humility and silence is all that's required. The throne adds dignity to our lives only by contrast to the servility all around. Without it, the throne is just a tatty old armchair. Other monarchs have different ideas of course. King Haakan of Norway was very democratic. When he stayed in the Palace, many's the laugh and joke he had with the servants at the Privy Purse door when he came to pick up his laundry. I can't see Prince Philip doing that. He knows we servants wouldn't like it.

Anyway I didn't have any more ideas. I just concentrated on mastering my job. As a consequence I rose from being General Footman and Keeper of the Third Door to Head Footman and Keeper of the First Door.

Let me explain what this means. It will give you a privileged insight into the intimate workings of our system of Monarchy. The Banqueting Hall at the Palace has three sets of doors. In going into the hall for a State Banquet, these doors are open and my job is merely to stand there, in my red and gold livery, with dainty knee-breeches and silk stockings, and look deferential. I just watch the Lord Chamberlain, the Chief Officer of the Court, lead the Royal procession from the private apartments. He is dressed in his ceremonial suit with a gold key hanging round his neck and he walks backwards, never taking his eyes off the Queen as trumpets sound and the Gentlemen-at-Arms in cream and gold, stand to attention and Her Majesty swinging her little handbag leads the procession into the hall.

During the meal the doors are closed. When they have finished, they rise and make their way towards the first door with the Queen in the lead. The Keeper of the First Door's moment has come. It's all up to him now. He has to open the door and let them out. That's an art I can tell you. It takes training but you also have to have a built-in sense of timing because the door has to be opened at exactly the right moment. Open it too soon and it would look as though you were showing Her Majesty out. Open it too late and she would be left standing in front of the closed door, shuffling from one foot to another. Worse she could come to a sudden halt in front of it and those behind her would walk straight into her regal back. There could be a royal pile-up of the good and the great.

The Keeper of the First Door is the key to the success of the whole process. I finally rose to that high position and I remember all too well my first outing in that capacity. It was a State Banquet for the Queen of the Netherlands. The eating was over, I was standing there ready to open the door for the assembly. But I found I was sweating so much I couldn't get a grip on the doorknob. It was a nightmare. I kept twisting but it kept slipping as the royal procession got nearer and nearer. Her Majesty loomed: she was almost on top of me when I finally got a grip on myself and the knob. I flung open the door and Her Gracious Majesty Queen Elizabeth II passed through. Her eyes flicked across at me, I think with approval. The timing was perfect.

It could've gone the other way. I could've embarrassed everybody. It happens more often than you think at the Palace. I remember when a lady of some repute was being presented to the Queen she curtsied and then couldn't get up. Her knee had locked. The Queen graciously pretended not to notice and passed on. It took two Footmen and a Porter to raise the woman. Very big for her age. Australian I believe.

When I first came to the Palace and worked as Keeper of the Third Door I was a slim slightly nervous figure. But respectability thickened me out. Now I have the weight and dignity that goes with the job. No more nervous gestures, my shoulders are broad, ready to push aside all obstacles.

Of course we courtiers get certain disabilities that go with the job. Like miners we suffer from chronic back pains. It comes from all the bowing we have to do. I always made sure my bows were strictly functional in contrast to all the florid bobbings that went on around me. Daily Body Control classes are now laid on to make spines more flexible. We were always having eye trouble too. That's brought on by us having to avert your eyes so much when we meet or talk to the Royals. We mustn't look them straight in the face. That's a ruling brought in during George's reign. He had a run-in with the Footman of the Bedchamber. George was creeping out for a nightcap and crashed straight into the Footman sending him flying. Next morning His Majesty had the Master of the Household up before him and raged on about the Footman's insolence. 'But what did he do Your Majesty?' 'Do? Do? He swore at me with his eyes!'

Since then the staff have had strict instructions not to look directly at the Royals. But it's a strain. What with bowing, looking down, and walking backwards, it's no wonder we develop physical disabilities. We're prone to other diseases too like pickled livers for example. That came about because of an old custom which laid it down that a bottle of whisky had to be provided every night for the Royal bedroom. That bottle was one of the perks of the King's Pages who usually retired early with advanced DTs. The custom was abolished during the war though everyone grumbled it was the thin end of the wedge.

But drinking is still the biggest occupational hazard of working at the Palace. There's so much of it about and so much time to drink it in. My friend Charles Twiggs former Keeper of the First Door was a big elbow bender. He'd spend his afternoons drinking at his favourite watering hole, the 'Court Circular' in Brewer Street. I often went with him. He liked company. That's how I moved up from Third to Second and finally to First Keeper. Charles' drinking was getting excessive even for a Footman. One particular afternoon we came out of the 'Circular' and there had been an accident. A small crowd had gathered round a man who had been knocked down and was sitting on the pavement. Twiggs swayed over to him and asked 'What is it?' The man replied, 'Accident. I think I've hurt my foot.' 'Right,' says Twiggs, 'Let me look at it.' 'Thank you. Are you a doctor?' 'No,' says Twiggs, 'a footman.'

They didn't appreciate that back at the Palace. I mentioned it to a colleague and somebody must've overheard. Have you noticed how large the Royal ears are in relation to the rest of their bodies? Anyway I suppose it was because of me old Twiggs got the push and I got his job. Funny thing that. I started off a small nobody, but I've made it. I've avoided thoughts, 'cause every thought makes trouble. I've learnt the

English values of obedience and humility. I don't want to assert my independence. People who do go bankrupt. I swim with the tide. Nothing disturbs me. I eat well, sleep better. Except I keep having this odd dream. I'm standing in a hall, crowned with filth, a crumb of dirt, guts and garbage, drips in a toilet pan. It's strange because I don't see myself like that. I've had a successful life any Englishman would be proud of, don't you think?